at a glance

WITHDRAWN

A quick guide to Children's Special Needs

Linda Evans & Viv East

Q
QUESTIONS
PUBLISHING

Questions Publishing, 27 Frederick Street, Hockley, Birmingham B1 3HH

The Questions Publishing Company Ltd
27 Frederick Street, Birmingham B1 3HH

First published in 2001

ISBN: 1-84190-069-9

Cover design by Ivan Morisson

Printed in the UK

Contents

Why 'at a glance'?

The answer is simple: to provide a quick reference point for busy teachers and classroom assistants. The inclusion of more SEN children in mainstream classes means that staff have to deal with a range of learning needs and/or medical conditions.

We can't all be experts but we can make sure that we have a basic understanding of pupils' difficulties in the classroom, and that we are armed with a range of practical strategies to help.

This book covers all of the most frequently encountered 'conditions' arranged alphabetically to enable quick access to the page required. There you will find:

● A brief introduction to the condition, including possible causes and prevalence
● An explanation of the main difficulties as they may manifest themselves in the classroom
● A range of practical strategies to adopt
● A useful address and/or website that can provide further information

Where appropriate, an example of a possible IEP is provided and a list of further contacts can be found at the back of the book.

The Individual Education Plans are there to give suggestions only as it is recognised that any IEP must be based on individual needs and that schools throughout the country operate different systems. The whole point of such a plan is that it is carefully designed for each individual child, and the new Code of Practice makes it clear that IEPs should set targets and suggest strategies that are additional to those expected for all pupils.

Throughout this book it is emphasised that each pupil is an individual and that the key to success lies in teaching on the basis of individual needs and individual preferences. Therefore, it is important that any IEP reflects 3 or 4 relevant, achievable targets together with an acknowledgement of the pupil's strengths so that these may be utilised. Everyone involved must learn from an IEP. Whatever approaches are used it is important to review frequently in order to assess success. Teachers sÌst be brave enough to change and try something new when the situation requires it, remembering that no single approach will work with all pupils, even if they experience similar difficulties.

Any IEP should be a working document that has a specific life span, so it is vital that a review date is planned and included.

Consultation with parents, relevant staff and, whenever possible, the pupil himself is essential. If everyone involved shares the same goals success is more likely.

INDIVIDUAL EDUCATION PLAN

Name:

Year:

Stage:

Area of concern: ADHD

Strengths: Likes to see finished work.

Teacher/Support:

Start date:

Review date:

IEP no.:

Targets:
1. To remain in his seat for at least 10 minutes.
2. To complete a task sheet for each lesson.
3. To achieve 5 rewards per week.
4. To work co-operatively with 1 other pupil.

Strategies for use in class:
1. Always maintain eye contact.
2. Make sure the task sheet contains short, easily achievable goals that will ensure success. More can be added once it is working well. In addition check that x understands what to do and takes responsibility for stamping when completed.
3. It is important that each lesson contains a variety of activities.
4. Use the 'time-out' room when necessary.
5. Encourage x to help with tasks between lesson times to cut down opportunities for problems with peers.
6. Use teacher attention to praise good, on task behaviour.

Role of Parent(s)/Carer(s):
1. Calm routines in the morning before school.
2. Consistent messages.
3. Weekly liaison with school.

Success Criteria:
1. To succeed with target on a gradual basis, beginning with 1 lesson, then 2 and so on.
2. Stars will be given for each time a target is hit.
3. x will work with one other pupil in PE and for Science.

Resources:
1. Guidelines for all staff provided.
2. Task sheet template on computer.
3. 'Time-out' room.
4. LSA for 10 hours per week.

Agreed by:

SENCO:

Parent(s)/Carer(s):

Pupil:

Date:

ADHD

Attention Deficit Hyperactivity Disorder is a term used to describe children who exhibit over-active behaviour and impulsivity and who have difficulty in paying attention. It is estimated that 0.5 – 1% of children in the UK are affected by ADHD, and about five times more boys than girls are diagnosed with this condition. Children of all levels of ability can have ADHD. Some professionals feel that the term is becoming over-used and extended to include any child who is naughty, but research points to a substantial number of children demonstrating a range of behaviours which constitute a diagnosis of ADHD. In some, more severe cases, the child may be treated with medication such as methylphenidate (Ritalin) which can have very beneficial effects but this remains a controversial issue.

Symptoms which characterise ADHD:

- difficulty in following instructions and completing tasks
- difficulty in 'sticking to' an activity
- easily distracted and forgetful
- often doesn't listen when spoken to
- fidgets, is restless, can't sit still
- interferes with other children's work
- can't stop talking, interrupts others
- runs about when inappropriate
- blurts out answers without waiting to be asked
- difficulty in waiting or taking turns
- acting impulsively without thinking about the consequences

Although most children will demonstrate some of these behaviours some of the time, those who have several of these problems consistently, at home and at school are likely to have ADHD. These children often find it hard to learn; research from the USA suggests that 90% of children with ADHD underachieve at school and 20% have reading difficulties.

How can we help?

If parents are given support while their children are young, they may be able to prevent problems later on. Some key principles are as follows:

- make eye contact with the child when speaking to him. If you call out from another room he will ignore you
- keep instructions simple – the one sentence rule
- give very specific praise, catch him being good
- keep calm – if you get angry the child will mirror that emotion
- use a 'quiet time' technique to deal with temper tantrums

- practise ways of distracting the child
- provide clear routines
- give advance warning when something is about to happen, or finish
- give two choices, avoiding the option of saying no: 'do you want to put your coat on now or when we get outside?'

Teachers and other school staff can help children with ADHD by careful consideration of how they organise the classroom and how they themselves behave:

- arrange the room to minimise distractions
- use a variety of activities in every lesson, alternating physical and sitting-down tasks
- set short, achievable targets and give instant rewards when the child completes tasks
- present text in large, well-spaced format without a lot of clutter on the page
- keep classroom rules clear and simple – and rehearse them regularly
- use checklists to help him work through a task or homework activity
- encourage the pupil to verbalise what needs to be done – first to the teacher then silently to himself
- use teacher attention and praise to reward positive behaviour
- give the pupil special responsibilities so that others see him in a positive light and he develops a positive self image

INDIVIDUAL EDUCATION PLAN

Name:

Year: 10

Stage:

Area of concern: Asperger's syndrome

Strengths: Rote learning

Teacher/Support:

Start date:

Review date:

IEP no.: 8

Targets:

1. To act as a helper in computer club.
2. To develop an understanding of metaphors – x will work on the meaning of 10 common metaphors.
3. To complete each days tasks and work sheet.

Strategies for use in class:

1. Remember to address x by name.
2. Make sure tasks are written down as well as explained so that x is prepared for what he has to do. Please remember to initial his worksheet.
3. Use x's strengths for remembering facts to boost self-esteem.
4. Use straightforward language.
5. Respect x's need for space and allow him to sit at the end of a row/desk.
6. Make use of computers whenever possible.

Role of Parent(s)/Carer(s):

1. To help with homework.
2. Regular contact with SENCO.
3. To reinforce work on metaphors.

Success Criteria:

1. To be seen helping younger pupils rather than sitting at the computer by himself on at least 5 separate occasions.
2. To be able to explain a given metaphor from the ones being studied.
3. To hand in his work sheet at the end of each day showing each task has been completed.

Resources:

1. Special pack in staff room for use/advice.
2. Daily worksheet – copy in staff room.
3. x has a buddy – this is ….
4. Use of 'time-out' room if needed.
5. Work with SENCO & SSA on social skills, how to help in computer club, etc.

Agreed by:

SENCO:

Parent(s)/Carer(s):

Pupil:

Date:

Asperger's Syndrome

Regarded by some as a distinctive condition, Asperger's Syndrome (AS) is viewed by others as the higher-ability aspect of the autistic spectrum. Individuals with AS can have symptoms ranging from mild to severe but tend to have serious difficulties with communication and social skills. Children often speak in a monotonous or exaggerated tone and at great length about topics which interest them. They avoid eye contact and often have obsessive, repetitive routines and preoccupations.

Because of their high degree of functionality and their naivite, those with AS are often thought of as 'odd', and are frequently a target for bullying. The causes of AS are still under investigation but research suggests that it may not be the result of a single factor but a series of neuro-biological triggers that affect brain development. Numbers affected are thought to be in the region of between 10 – 36 in every 10,000; with more males than females affected.

The main characteristics:

- **Difficulties with social relationships.** They find it difficult to read the signals which most of us take for granted and find it hard to interact with others.
- **Difficulties with communication.** They may speak very fluently but not take much notice of the reaction of people listening to them; they may talk on and on regardless of the listener's interest or may appear insensitive to their feelings. Despite having good language skills, people with Asperger syndrome may sound over-precise or over-literal – jokes can cause problems as can exaggerated language and metaphors; for example, a person with Asperger syndrome may be confused or frightened by a statement like 'she bit my head off'.
- **Difficulties with social imagination, imaginative play and flexible thinking.** While they often excel at learning facts and figures, people with Asperger syndrome find it hard to think in abstract ways. This can cause problems for children in school where they may have difficulty with certain subjects, such as literature or religious studies.

The child may also be:

- socially awkward and clumsy in relations with other children and/or adults
- naive and gullible
- often unaware of others' feelings
- unable to carry on a 'give and take' conversation
- easily upset by changes in routines and transitions
- literal in speech and understanding
- overly sensitive to loud sounds, lights or odours
- fixated on one subject or object
- physically awkward in sports

They may have:

- unusually accurate memory for details
- sleeping or eating problems
- trouble understanding things they have heard or read
- inappropriate body language or facial expression
- unusual speech patterns (repetitive and/or irrelevant remarks)
- stilted, formal manner of speaking
- unusually loud, high or monotonous voice
- tendency to rock, fidget or pace while concentrating

How can we help?

- Talk to parents!
- Be flexible
- Prepare them for any changes well in advance – have a contingency plan for emergencies. At school, they may get upset by sudden changes, such as an alteration to the timetable
- Have high expectations
- Use their ability to remember by rote to increase self esteem
- Always refer to the pupil by name – they do not necessarily realise that 'everyone' includes them
- Be calm – never shout
- Modify facial expressions and body language – ensure the child has time to respond
- Be precise with instructions, e.g. 'we are going outside now' not 'shall we go outside?'
- Use concrete apparatus
- Use visual lists, e.g. a daily timetable
- Present small, manageable tasks with visual prompts
- Acknowledge the need for personal space, e.g. allow them to sit on the end of the row in assembly
- Provide a place for time out when they need it
- Keep to a structured classroom – use labels, specific areas for specific tasks
- Apply rules consistently
- Develop a buddy system if possible
- Use stories to teach communication /social interaction
- Ensure everyone who comes into contact with the child knows how to react, e.g. lunch-time supervisors, supply staff
- Make good use of computers – they are not demanding in emotional terms, as people often are

http://www.oneworld.org/autism_uk/
http://www.aspennj.org
National Autistic Society
393 City Road
London EC1V 1NG Tel: 020 7833 2299

INDIVIDUAL EDUCATION PLAN

Name:

Year: 1

Stage:

Area of concern: Autistic Spectrum Disorder

Strengths: Rote memory, interest in cars

Teacher/Support: LSA x 2hours per day

Start date:

Review date:

IEP no.: 3

Targets:

1. To sit still and quietly in assembly.
2. To sit on the carpet appropriately during literacy & numeracy.
3. To be the milk monitor for his table.
4. To play constructively with up to 2 peers at playtime.

Strategies for use in class:

1. Always address *x* by name.
2. Always give clear, simple instructions.
3. Use a visual timetable and task list.
4. Make use of *x*'s interest in cars to make word cards, number lines, etc.
5. Make use of this interest to encourage social interaction.
6. Use this interest to give rewards.
7. Keep to routines – if there is going to be a change prepare *x* well in advance.
8. Keep interested through a variety of tasks.
9. Make use of *x*'s memory in mental Maths.

Role of Parent(s)/Carer(s):

1. Daily contact through 'home/class' book.
2. Daily reading.

Success Criteria:

1. Will be able to sit in assembly like his peers.
2. Increasing time spent appropriately beginning with 5 minutes and escalating.
3. To carry out 'monitor' duties without reminders.
4. To play with LSA supervision in the first instance; LSA gradually withdrawing to a distance.

Resources:

1. A square of carpet for use in assembly and during literacy and numeracy to create a clear boundary.
2. Clear labels on all equipment using pictures and symbols.
3. Visual timetable and task lists.
4. Social stories – see Advisor.
5. Use of spinning tops, skittles, etc. for playtime.

Agreed by:

SENCO:

Parent(s)/Carer(s):

Pupil:

Date:

Autistic Spectrum
Disorder

A utism is a pervasive developmental disorder and since the 1980s the idea of a 'spectrum of autistic disorders' has been widely acknowledged.

The causes of autism are complex and it is unlikely that there is a single cause, but rather a set of triggers involving biological/medical, psychological and behavioural factors. There appears to be a strong genetic link.

Psychological assessments can be helpful but they cannot be used to confirm or deny a diagnosis of ASD. The diagnosis is medical and is made by recognising patterns of behaviour from early life which indicate impairment of social interaction, communication and development of imagination. This is known as the 'Triad of Impairments'.

At one end of the spectrum will be a normally intelligent child with mild autism, and at the other end will be the child with profound learning difficulties and severe autism. The estimated prevalence of ASD is 6:1000 and it affects four times as many boys as girls.

What are the main characteristics?

● **Social Interaction**

The child will have an inability to empathise with others and will find it difficult to understand the feelings and/or behaviour of others. They may appear withdrawn and make little attempt to make friends, often being described as 'aloof'. Sometimes their behaviour is odd – using inappropriate greetings, touching or being aggressive.

Children with ASD have difficulties understanding and interpreting social situations and may become distressed or confused.

● **Communication**

This includes a difficulty in making sense of and using both verbal and non-verbal communication such as eye contact, facial expression, gesture and body language.

Some children never develop speech; others experience a significant language delay and when they do begin to use language it is often repetitive and/or learned phrases from things such as television cartoons or adverts.

In contrast, some children appear to have good expressive language but still have difficulties in understanding and tend to interpret literally.

● **Thought and Imagination**

An impairment in thought and imagination affects every area of thinking, language and behaviour.

In Early Years settings an impairment in play and imaginative activities is often noticeable. Children may become fixated by a particular toy, especially one that spins and shines. They may develop repetitive and/or obsessive interests and are often more interested in objects than people.

Changes in routine can cause distress because ASD children are dependent upon routine to make sense of their environment.

Additional Difficulties

In addition to the 'triad of impairments' children with ASD may experience any number of the following:

● Hand flapping, rocking or spinning
● Sensitivity to noise, smell, taste, touch or visual stimuli
● Erratic sleeping patterns
● Unusual eating habits
● Self injury
● Aggressive behaviour
● Hyperactivity
● A strange gait or posture – often walking on tip-toes
● Irrational fears or phobias

About 10% have a special creative or mathematical skill such as remembering dates or making complicated mathematical calculations.

How can we help?

● Have a structured classroom – use labels & specific areas for specific tasks
● Provide an individual work area – acknowledge the need for personal space
● Use a visual timetable and task lists
● Consider lighting, noise, etc.
● Introduce only **one** skill at a time
● Be positive and patient – keep **calm** and be flexible
● Always refer to the child by name – they may not realise 'everyone' includes them
● Use obsessions as rewards and encourage interaction through activities they enjoy
● Teach them to recognise behaviours, emotions, body language
● Do not expect eye contact and **never** turn their face to look at you
● Keep verbal instructions brief and simple
● Use stories to teach social communication/interaction
● Teach jokes, puns and metaphors
● Disapprove of inappropriate behaviour **not** the child
● Provide clear boundaries for behaviour
● Prepare for changes in advance
● Develop a 'buddy' system
● Make good use of computers
● Have high expectations
● Always talk to parents

National Autistic Society
www.nas.org.uk
email: nas@mailbox.ulcc.ac.uk

Centre for the study of autism:
www.autism.org/contents.html

INDIVIDUAL EDUCATION PLAN

Name:

Year: 4

Stage:

Area of concern: Cerebral Palsy & mild learning difficulties.

Strengths: Determination

Teacher/Support: 15 hours LSA

Start date:

Review date:

IEP no.:

Role of Parent(s)/Carer(s):
1. Regular liaison between home and school – use of 'home/school' book.
2. Help with reading and spelling games, 15 minutes after tea Mon, Tues, Wed, Thur.

Targets:
1. To complete set physiotherapy programme.
2. To complete at least 2 readers per week.
3. To learn 15 more words from NLS, Year 1-2 (see literacy record book for specifics) for both reading and spelling.
4. To complete the 'core' activities from each lesson.

Strategies for use in class:
1. Ensure x can manoeuvre successfully within the classroom – ensure clutter free aisles.
2. Use a buddy system for help at break, lunch and in PE.
3. Set 'core' targets for completion in lessons bearing in mind the possible need for extra time.
4. Use a sloping writing desk.
5. Make good use of computer aids – as advised by the OT.
6. Use ALS games for help with reading/spelling tasks.

Success Criteria:
1. As assessed by the physiotherapist.
2. Evidence in the reading diary.
3. Successful reading and spelling of the words on at least 3 occasions.
4. Completion of 'core' activities.

Resources:
1. Advice and help from both the physiotherapist and the OT – see reports.
2. 15 hours LSA time.
3. Computer aids located in x's classroom – see *Ms. ?* for guidance on use.
4. ALS games and multi-sensory learning aids.
5. Sloping desk for writing tasks.

Agreed by:

SENCO:

Parent(s)/Carer(s):

Pupil:

Date:

Cerebral Palsy (cp)

Cerebral palsy is a general term for a wide range of non-progressive cerebral (brain) disorders. It is a persistent disorder of movement and posture and occurs when part of the brain is not working properly or has not developed. This happens before birth, at birth or during early childhood, in other words before the brain's growth has reached a certain level of maturity. The affected part of the brain usually controls muscles and certain movements and cp results in jumbled messages between the brain and the muscles. It is estimated that one in 400 children are affected. No two people with cp are the same and the term covers the full spectrum, from those where it is barely noticeable to those who are severely affected.

Types of Cerebral Palsy

Spastic – this is an impairment of the cerebral cortex and is the most common form of cp. Spastic means 'stiff' and those with spastic cp have stiffened muscles and decreased movement in their joints.

● Hemiplegia – one side of the body affected
● Diplegia – legs affected more than arms
● Quadriplegia – arms and legs both affected

Athetoid – an impairment of the basal ganglia. This is where the muscles rapidly change from floppy to tense resulting in involuntary movements. Speech can be hard to understand because those affected have difficulty controlling their tongue, breathing and vocal chords. Hearing problems can also occur.

Ataxic – this is rare and caused by impairment in the cerebellum. Those with ataxic cp find it difficult to balance and have poor spatial awareness. The whole of the body is affected and although they can walk they may be unsteady. In addition they may experience shaky hand movements and jerky speech.

The effects of cp vary so much, it is often difficult to diagnose which type of cp is present and many people have a combination of types. It is also difficult to predict how a child's independence will be affected in later life. Cerebral palsy is not progressive although some difficulties may become more noticeable as the child gets older. There is no cure but good positioning, early play and physiotherapy can improve posture and muscle control.

Therapy

Therapists and Educational Psychologists play an important part in assessing a child's needs and in advising the best ways of promoting development:

● Speech & Language Therapy
● Occupational Therapy/Physiotherapy
● Conductive Education
● Bobath Therapy
● Botulinum Toxin A

Associated difficulties

A child with cp may not have any associated difficulties but staff in school need to bear in mind the possibility of problems with:

● Sleeping
● Constipation
● Speech and understanding the spoken word
● Epilepsy
● Visual perception
● Learning difficulties – moderate to severe
● Specific learning difficulties (specific parts of the brain affected)

Inclusion

Early school experiences can have a profound effect on how people feel about themselves and influence their expectations about their future role in society. It is important that the education experience is a positive one for all children, but especially those with a disability. Being included, or having regular contact with mainstream peers can improve youngsters' confidence and raise their aspirations. It also means that non-disabled children learn to accept people with 'differences' and how to accommodate them in society.

How can we help?

● Talk to parents
● Co-ordinate the work of all relevant specialist/therapists
● Think about physical access – ramps, lifts, toilets, classroom layout
● Think about curriculum access – teaching styles, learning objectives, appropriate support, allowing extra time
● Use a 'buddy' system
● Make use of ICT – the LEA advisor may be able to help (*Inclusive Technology* and *Semerc* are specialist providers)
● Make use of audio-visual aids
● Promote 'difference' through PSHE

Remember, someone who is severely physically affected may be of average or above average intelligence!

www.scope.org.uk Scope, 6 Market Road, London N7 9PW
www.conductive-education.org.uk
tel: 0121 449 1569
www.inclusive.co.uk tel: 01457 819790
www.semerc.com tel: 0161 827 2927

INDIVIDUAL EDUCATION PLAN

Name:

Year: 8

Stage:

Area of concern: organisational difficulties, social skills

Strengths: individual work, with clear targets

Teacher/Support: LSA for two hours every day

Start date:

Review date:

IEP no.:

Targets:

1. To arrive at lessons with appropriate books and equipment.
2. To buy and eat lunch in the dining hall with one of three 'buddies'.
3. To contribute to group work in English lessons.

Strategies for use in class:

1. Remember to praise J for bringing the appropriate books and equipment to lessons (and write a comment in his Personal Work Record).
2. Make sure he writes in his PWR appropriate reminders for next lesson (e.g. ingredients for food technology).
3. Give J clear targets for each lesson, (these may be different to those for other pupils in terms of length of pieces of writing etc.).
4. Encourage J to work with other pupils as well as his LSA. As he prefers to work on his own, offer this opportunity as an incentive, "work with B on this experiment and talk to him about what happens; then you can fill in the work sheet on your own".
5. In group work, ensure that J has a clear role within the group and understands what is expected of him.

Role of Parent(s)/Carer(s):

1. To check J's PWR every day and ensure that a) homework is completed on time, b) books/equipment are ready for the following day.
2. To allow J to bring home a friend after school one evening per week.
3. To pass on to J any positive feedback from staff.

Success Criteria:

1. To increase the number of positive comments form subject teachers in J's Personal Work Record (Currently two from a possible twenty-five).
2. To be seen sitting with other pupils in the dining hall and eating lunch in an acceptable manner.
3. To accept a given role within a group in English lessons, and (with support from LSA) to contribute to the joint effort.

Resources:

1. Wherever possible, inform the LSA of work to be covered in the next lesson – she may design an alternative worksheet or method of recording.
2. J to see the SENCo every day before afternoon registration, to discuss his lunchtime behaviour and give positive reinforcement where appropriate.
3. Attendance at the lunch-time study club to read with a 'buddy', play spelling games etc.

Agreed by:

SENCO:

Parent(s)/Carer(s):

Pupil:

Date:

Down's Syndrome

Down's syndrome is a genetic disorder and occurs when a baby is born with an additional chromosome, (47 instead of 46). It is the most common form of learning disability, occurring in about 1 of every 1000 live births a year. Children with Down's syndrome are not just generally delayed in their development: they have a specific learning profile with characteristic strengths and weaknesses.

Many schools are now welcoming children with Down's syndrome into the mainstream and increased involvement with their non-disabled peers, coupled with higher expectations from teachers, means that children are achieving far more – both socially and educationally.

What are the main characteristics?

There are specific physical features associated with the condition and children may have problems such as eye defects, respiratory problems and heart defects. Learning difficulties range from moderate to severe.

The following factors are typical of many children with Down's syndrome. Some have physical implications, others have cognitive ones; some have both.

- Delayed motor skills – fine and gross
- Auditory and visual impairment
- Speech and language impairment
- Poor auditory memory
- Limited concentration span
- Difficulties with thinking and reasoning, and applying knowledge to new situations
- Sequencing difficulties

Like all children with special needs, those with Down's syndrome need to be treated as individuals. There is a wide variety of measurable ability within this group, which makes generalisation difficult. Many children grow up to lead independent lives within their community, holding down a job and enjoying a lasting relationship.

How can we help?

There is no definitive guide to good practice and teachers are often confused about how to respond to these youngsters in the classroom. Often, they link inappropriate behaviour to the child's label and believe that it can't be challenged or managed; the tendency is to be over-protective and lenient.

Working alongside parents, sharing practice and experience with colleagues and involving the youngsters themselves in planning and decision-making, constitute the foundation of good provision.

- Nominate a key person in school to be the first point of contact if there is a problem
- Teach timetable, routines and school rules explicitly, allowing time to learn them
- Make sure the rules are clear and apply them to pupils with Down's syndrome alongside their peers
- Speak directly to the pupil and reinforce what you say with facial expression, pictures and concrete materials
- Use simple and familiar language and short sentences
- Give the child time to process language and form a response
- Listen carefully – your ear will adjust
- Ensure consistency of approach by all teachers and non-teaching staff
- Use short, clear instructions and check understanding
- Provide additional practice to develop motor skills
- Distinguish the 'can't do' from the 'won't do'
- Consider any inappropriate behaviour in terms of 'why did this happen?' Check whether: the pupil understands the task
  the task is too hard or too easy
  the materials used are too babyish
  the task is too long
- For a younger child make an activity box for times when he finishes an activity before his peers, needs a change of task or 'time out'. Put in books, fine-motor skills activities etc. Allow another child to join in as a way of encouraging social interaction
- Provide lots of short listening activities and use visual/tactile materials to reinforce oral work
- Set up regular and frequent opportunities for the pupil to speak to others (both peers and adults)
- Ignore attention-seeking behaviour within reasonable limits
- Remember that the classteacher has ultimate responsibility for the child (the LSA should not be the only adult dealing with him or her)
- Be aware that too much one-to-one support can be counter-productive
- Make sure the pupil is working with others who are good role models

The Down's Association, 155, Mitcham Road, London SW17 9PG
www.downs-syndrome.org.uk
www.sdsa.org.uk

INDIVIDUAL EDUCATION PLAN

Name:

Year: 3

Stage:

Area of concern: Dyscalculia

Strengths: Art, oral work, reading

Teacher/Support: LSA for Numeracy & Science groups

Start date:

Review date:

IEP no.: 2

Targets:

1. To be able to name a triangle, rectangle and hexagon.
2. To be able to compute numbers up to 20 using addition and subtraction.
3. To be able to make a simple tally chart.
4. To answer at least 1 question during the oral part of the Numeracy hour.

Strategies for use in class:

1. Use multi-sensory learning methods concentrating on just one shape at a time and do not move on until that shape is secure.
2. Make sure the calculations are written in x's book in advance; leave a clear space between and put a green dot above the units column to remind x that this is where to start. Ensure that concrete apparatus is available.
3. Use the computer program. On paper encourage the use of different colours. Make sure that when first teaching, the concrete example is available.
4. Ask the same question of another member of the class directly before x. As x becomes more confident leave a gap. Always make sure the question is within the work x has covered.

Role of Parent(s)/Carer(s):

1. To play the Snakes & Ladders shape game.
2. Encourage x to see number in everyday life – booklet provided with suggestions.

Success Criteria:

1. Successfully naming these shapes on at least three separate occasions.
2. Consistent success with computations.
3. For x to be able to make a simple tally chart without assistance.
4. For x to feel comfortable answering questions during the oral session. (Demonstrated by volunteering answers.)

Resources:

1. Group work with the LSA during Numeracy Hour and one Science session if needed.
2. Concrete shapes to feel and draw around, various worksheets, jigsaws, sand tray, computer programme, the Snakes & Ladders Shape game dice.
3. LSA time to write calculations in x's book in advance. Use of Cuisennaire or cubes as preferred by x.
4. Computer program, box of resources for concrete apparatus, boxes of pasta, coloured pens/pencils.

Agreed by:

SENCO:

Parent(s)/Carer(s):

Pupil:

Date:

Dyscalculia

Dyscalculia is one of a group of specific learning difficulties. It is a specific learning disability in Mathematics. It should not be confused with dyslexia, which is a difficulty with words. In fact students can be gifted in other academic areas but be confounded by Maths.

What are the causes?

There are several possibilities that have been put forward for the causes of dyscalculia including problems that occur at the foetal stage so that part of the brain is not 'wired up' correctly. In addition it has been acknowledged that fear and poor instruction could also play a large part.

Types

There are 2 main types of dyscalculia:

Developmental Dyscalculia – this is where there is a marked discrepancy between a person's developmental level and general cognitive ability on measures of specific Maths ability.

Dyscalculia – a total inability to abstract or consider concepts and numbers.

What to look for

It will take some observation and gathering of evidence to imply that dyscalculia is the problem rather than a single mathematical concept that has not been grasped. Difficulties may include:

- An inability to learn to count by rote
- Difficulty reading and/or writing the numbers
- Inconsistent computation results
- Omissions
- Reversals
- Transpositions
- Poor mental Maths
- An inability to grasp and remember mathematical concepts, rules and formulae
- Difficulty with time and time management
- Problems with sequencing – this can affect many things including problems with team games and dance sequences
- Poor sense of direction
- A poor memory for lay-out
- Confusion with left and right
- Stress at lesson change-over times
- Difficulties with games – they may lose track of whose turn it is
- Cannot remember names or faces
- Difficulties with money

There are a number of specific tests that can be used to identify dyscalculia and the Educational Psychologist should be able to help with this in school.

What can we do to help?

As with most strategies used to help those with special needs, these approaches will benefit all pupils.

- The first thing to do is find out what type of learner they are: grasshopper or inchworm
- Ask a child to explain how they have come to an answer – sometimes it may seem a little bizarre but if they understand it that way and it is mathematically workable, accept this
- Always explain a new concept step-by-step
- Encourage the child to teach it back to check they have understood
- Use concrete apparatus – some children may never move from this stage – these days there is a wealth of material that can be purchased, from bright plastic pies to teach fractions to large dice for playing games
- Use picture and visual stimuli
- Use multi-sensory methods – for example use the sand tray to trace numbers just as you would letters – make Maths as practical as possible
- Carefully teach the language and syntax of Maths
- Use number stories to help
- Encourage spaces between sums on a page – make sure the work is uncluttered and clearly set out
- If there is a problem copying numbers down accurately either from a book or the board make sure these are already in their book or folder
- Make use of the computer
- Make use of a calculator – some children may always struggle so we must encourage and teach them to use the tools that can do the job for them
- Acknowledge the trauma that these children experience with Maths
- Allow extra time – this will be important in stressful times such as tests or examinations
- Encourage the use of rough paper to work out calculations
- Use wall displays with each of the 4 symbols in the middle and all the words used to mean that around the outside
- For older pupils use a credit card holder to keep reminders of formulae, tables, etc.
- Make good use of mnemonics to help remember sequences, for example 'Damned Silly Triangle'
- Encourage peer support for getting round the school, changing lessons, etc.
- For older pupils, ensure someone will help with organisation at exam time

www.dyscalculia.co.uk

INDIVIDUAL EDUCATION PLAN

Name:

Year: 8

Stage:

Area of concern: Dyslexia/Sp.L.D.

Strengths: Oral work, Art, D&T

Teacher/Support:

Targets:
1. To be able to use syllabification to aid spelling of 10 regular words.
2. To learn to use mind maps for recording and revision.
3. To remember correct books, equipment, etc. for lessons.

Start date:

Review date:

IEP no.: 2

Strategies for use in class:
1. Provide key word lists for each subject.
2. Encourage alternative methods of recording/revising, e.g. mind maps.
3. Use *x's* strengths to explore understanding.
4. Help to make sure *x* has his/her homework recorded correctly – encourage buddy system.
5. Remember to allow extra time!
6. Praise for having appropriate books and equipment.

Role of Parent(s)/Carer(s):
1. Encourage with organisation and homework – visual reminders on door and in bedroom.
2. 10 minutes x 3 per week to go through spellings.

Success Criteria:
1. Can demonstrate syllabification to aid spelling of 6 regular words on 3 separate occasions.
2. Can explain and demonstrate how to use mind maps.
3. Has correct books and equipment for all lessons – as recorded by subject teachers on record sheet provided.

Resources:
1. Alpha to Omega, jigwords, etc. for use in spelling sessions.
2. Information sheet on mind maps.
3. Credit card holder for key words.
4. Visual reminder for timetable and organisation.
5. Tick sheet for teachers to record x having correct books etc. in lessons.

Agreed by:

SENCO:

Parent(s)/Carer(s):

Pupil:

Date:

Dyslexia

The literal translation of the word 'dyslexia' is '*difficulty with words*'. It can affect an individual's ability to read quickly and efficiently and nearly always results in poor or 'bizarre' spellings. Pupils with dyslexia often have poor short-term memory and difficulty with sequencing and processing information – skills which are important for effective learning in a busy classroom.

There has been a great deal of research and numerous attempts to define dyslexia. The British Dyslexia Association (BDA) defines it as 'a complex neurological condition which is constitutional in origin …' Magnetic Resonance Imaging (MRI) has been used to identify specific areas of the brain involved in reading and preliminary results indicate less activity in certain areas in people with dyslexia. Dyslexia is perhaps best summed up as a syndrome with a wide range of possible causes and symptoms. Although found across the whole range of cognitive ability, the idea that dyslexia presents as a discrepancy between expected outcomes and performance, is still widely held.

Numbers affected vary according to the definitions used, but it is generally accepted that between 5 – 10% of the population is affected to some degree. Many dyslexics may be helped through systematic hard work and appropriate interventions, especially when identified early.

What are the main characteristics?

Reading
Many dyslexics describe a page of print as moving or swirling and experience tracking difficulties, frequently losing their place. Poor phonological processing leads to difficulties with blending and segmenting. It can be frustrating to listen to a dyslexic read as they may make frequent errors with high frequency words but seem able to cope with those that are more complicated. Some believe this is because they need to visualise as they read and many of the high-frequency words do not lend themselves to easy visualisation (the, and, when). Whilst many dyslexic children learn to read at a functional level, they remain slow and the activity requires a great deal of effort.

Writing
The written work of dyslexics is often of a poor standard compared with their oral ability. Their work can appear messy with frequent crossings out and several attempts at a single word. They tend to confuse similar letter shapes such as b/d/p/q, m/w, n/u and often make anagrams of words, e.g. tired/tried. Early spelling attempts can be 'bizarre' and this usually remains an area of difficulty into adult life.

General difficulties
● Speed of processing
● Poor short-term memory
● Sequencing
● Organisation
● Tiredness
● Uneven performance profile
● Behaviour – often a result of frustration

Strengths
Research has come up with a list of attributes that many dyslexics appear to have in greater abundance than non-dyslexics. This includes some form of creativity, whether it is in the form of Art, Drama, Music or Architecture. Others excel in individual sports such as swimming and many are known for their powers of lateral thinking.

How can we help?
● Work from their areas of strength
● Use a multi-sensory programme of teaching and learning
● Make use of pictures, plans, flow charts
● Pictorial timetables can be a great help
● Use videos, tapes and dictaphones and encourage alternative ways of recording
● Make use of ICT – voice recognition software can be a boon
● Teach study skills from an early age – the use of mind-maps has proved particularly successful
● Provide key word lists and displays
● Encourage the use of line trackers, book marks and/or coloured overlays as appropriate
● Keep board work to a minimum
● Tackle spelling patterns using methods such as Simultaneous Oral Spelling
● Teach a structured, cumulative phonic programme
● Allow sufficient **TIME** for all activities
● Use lots of **PRAISE**
● Ensure it is a whole school issue!

Each individual is unique and the key to success lies in teaching on the basis of individual needs and individual preferences.

The British Dyslexia Association
Tel: 0118 966 8271 www.bda-dyslexia.org.uk

Dyslexia Institute
Tel: 01784 463 851 www.dyslexia-inst.org.uk

INDIVIDUAL EDUCATION PLAN

Name:	**Area of concern:** Dyspraxia
Year: 1	**Strengths:** Keen to do well.
Stage:	**Teacher/Support:**

Start date:	
Review date:	
IEP no.:	

Targets:
1. To use and understand prepositions: in, behind, on, under.
2. To get dressed after PE on her own.
3. To take turns in a game with 1 other pupil.
4. To establish a pencil grip.

Strategies for use in class:
1. Give clear, short instructions.
2. Arrange a buddy system.
3. Have a card showing the order for getting dressed.
4. Use lots of practical activities such as peg-boards, painting, etc.
5. Make sure seating is correct – feet must be on the ground.
6. Have a range of pencil grips, chunky crayons and pencils for use.
7. Use gentle reminders to keep on task.
8. Use green/red dots to remind which way to work across the page.

Role of Parent(s)/Carer(s):
1. To encourage ✓/to dress herself in the morning.
2. To help with using cutlery.
3. To reinforce work on prepositions (e.g. read books like 'Where Is Spot?', ask ✓/to look 'behind' the sofa for hidden toys etc. [Hide and seek games])

Success Criteria:
1. Can demonstrate use of and understanding of the words on at least 3 separate occasions.
2. Gets clothes on in the right order.
3. Can play co-operatively with another pupil with at least 3 different games and on at least 5 different occasions.
4. Using a consistent grip and hand.

Resources:
1. Sloping board for desk.
2. A variety of pencil grips, pencils, etc.
3. Large arrows on walls to remind her which way to go, e.g. from peg to classroom.
4. 'Language Gap' games.
5. 15 minutes x 3 per week to work on language programme.
6. Carpet square to help positioning for literacy and numeracy hours.

Agreed by:

SENCO:

Parent(s)/Carer(s):

Pupil:

Date:

Dyspraxia

Dyspraxia is an immaturity in the way the brain processes information, resulting in messages not being properly transmitted. Children with dyspraxia may have problems with co-ordinating their movements, (in some cases, this extends to difficulties in co-ordinating the mouth and tongue, resulting in speech impairment), perception and thought.

Approximately 1 in 20 children have the condition to some degree, with boys affected four times more frequently than girls.

The signs of dyspraxia are often noticed by parents early on and may include problems with:

- achieving normal milestones such as sitting up, crawling, walking
- limited ability to concentrate
- picking up small objects
- language acquisition
- doing a jig-saw or sorting game
- holding a pencil
- understanding spatial concepts of in/on/behind etc.

In the classroom, the child with dyspraxia will come across numerous difficulties:

- games lessons (particularly where throwing and catching are involved), and music and movement classes
- following sequential instructions
- getting dressed, tying laces
- handwriting

- using a knife and fork
- confusion with laterality, with child changing between left and right hands
- an inability to recognise potential danger e.g. jumping from the top of the climbing frame, or for older pupils, using bunsen burners and other equipment in science and technology

In addition, children may demonstrate general irritability and limited social skills; they may tire easily and need periods of rest. Older pupils may have poor posture and limited body awareness, moving awkwardly and seeming clumsy.

How can we help?

- give extra supervision and encouragement to stay on task
- give clear and unambiguous instructions and check the pupil's understanding (dyspraxic children may not understand sarcasm or irony)
- make sure that the child's seating allows him to rest both feet on the floor, with the desk or table at elbow height and ideally, with the facility for a sloping surface to work on
- position the child where he has a direct view of the teacher and minimal distractions
- limit the amount of handwriting he is expected to do by providing printed sheets or offering alternative means of recording
- where pen and paper have to be used, try attaching the paper to the desk so that it doesn't have to be held still
- break down activities into small steps
- limit the amount of copying from the board; when necessary, use colours and appropriate 'chunking' to help him follow the text
- allow extra time for finishing work
- teach the pupil strategies to help him remember things and to be able to organise himself
- be aware that growth spurts may accentuate problems
- in games and outdoor activities be sensitive to the child's limitations and allocate a position/activity which offers the best chance of success
- encourage a partner relationship with another child who can help with tricky situations
- give extra praise and encouragement

With appropriate support and encouragement, dyspraxic children can do very well at school; talk to the parents – they may have found their own solutions to many of the problems.

Dyspraxic Foundation,
8 West Alley, Hitchin, Herts SG5 1EG
Tel: 01462 454986
www.emmbrook.demon.co.uk/dysprax/homepage.htm

INDIVIDUAL EDUCATION PLAN

Name:

Year: 3

Stage:

Area of concern: Fragile X

Strengths: Reading (though mechanical)

Teacher/Support: LSA

Start date:

Review date:

IEP no.:

Role of Parent(s)/Carer(s):
1. Regular liaison with class teacher.
2. Reinforce quiet times.
3. Play games with grandma for 10 minutes every Monday and Wednesday after school.

Targets:
1. To line up quietly for dinner.
2. To remain seated for 10 minute intervals.
3. To learn to take turns with 1-2 other children in a game.
4. To be able to add and take away tens and units.

Strategies for use in class:
1. Arrange for x to be first in the line accompanied by LSA. When achieved try another position in line but prepare first.
2. Use star charts, visual prompts, keep to same place in class – preferably quiet with only 2-3 other children close by and near to the teacher.
3. Work with LSA in small group using various literacy and numeracy games, including working at the computer.
4. Start from success point – see records, use practical apparatus.
5. Be firm but use lots of praise and rewards.
6. Use of quiet place for time out.

Success Criteria:
1. Demonstrating lining up quietly with the LSA.
2. Begin with achieving twice in 2 sessions a day and build up gradually.
3. To play literacy and numeracy games in a small group.
4. To complete written tasks.

Resources:
1. Playing-card-size visual prompts for lining up, sitting still, putting up hand, sitting quietly in assembly.
2. Lotto, Fishing, Dice, Diennes, etc. for games.
3. Star charts, certificates.
4. A quiet corner for respite.

Agreed by:

SENCO:

Parent(s)/Carer(s):

Pupil:

Date:

Fragile X Syndrome

Fragile X Syndrome is the most common form of inherited learning disability and is caused by a defect in the X chromosome. It is a strongly heritable condition with the possibility that an affected gene may become more affected as it is passed on from one generation to the next. The range of effects is wide and it is not possible to predict from a diagnosis of Fragile X, which features a child will show or to what degree he or she will be affected in terms of intellectual impairment and emotional and behavioural problems.

Fragile X can affect both males and females and both can be carriers. It is estimated that one in three thousand is affected and males are more often, and typically more severely, affected than females. Many Fragile X children and adults remain undiagnosed.

What are the main characteristics?

● Early years

In the early years, children with Fragile X may be 'floppy' and developmental milestones may be delayed. Gross and fine motor co-ordination remain poor and this affects handwriting.

● Speech and Language

Children who have Fragile X may have clear, relevant language or no language at all. They may suffer from difficulties with sound articulation and/or fluency. This in turn can lead to rapid speech rates, use of jargon and a litany-like phraseology. You may often hear them repeat the last word or phrase spoken to them or that they have spoken themselves. Conversation can be strained as they may frequently digress.

● Cognitive development

The verbal skills of children with Fragile X tend to be better than their reasoning skills. These strengths can lead to relative strengths in other areas such as reading. However, the difficulties with reasoning may mean that number concepts and processes present a problem area.

● Behaviour

This can range from a little impulsivity to disruptive outbursts and over activity. Children may rush around being unable to settle for long at any one activity and often act without thinking. At times of stress, a child may show anxiety through obsessions such as hand-flapping and can be persistent in his attention-seeking.

● Emotional factors

Children with Fragile X do not generally like 'busy' environments and they can be easily overwhelmed. They may find noises and smells upsetting and may react emotionally to relatively minor upsets. They can be over-sensitive to imagined criticism and have a need for security, routine and constant reassurance.

How can we help?

We can lessen anxieties of children who have Fragile X syndrome and improve their performance by looking at what situations we put them in and ensuring any intervention is related to the child's needs.

● Work with parents. Share ideas and strategies with them
● Use straightforward language/instructions
● Teach from the point the child has reached and make goals realistic
● Make the learning situation clear and uncluttered
● Keep to routines as far as possible and make sure any changes are prepared for and explained
● Aims and outcomes must be clear to the child
● Set positive objectives for change when dealing with behaviour
● Nip bad habits and/or obsessions in the bud
● Demands must be enforced
● Use lots of positive feedback and praise, making it clear that you are rewarding a particular behaviour
● Keep records, so that successful strategies can be revisited and shared with other staff

The key to effective intervention is the context in which the child lives: 'significant adults' – parents and carers, teachers and support assistants, need to work with consistency in promoting change and development in the child.

Fragile X Society (UK) 01424 813147
www.fragilex.org.uk

National Fragile X Foundation (USA)
www.nfxf.org

FRAXA Research Foundation (USA)
www.fraxa.org

INDIVIDUAL EDUCATION PLAN

Name:

Year: 3

Stage:

Area of concern: Hearing, Literacy

Strengths: Maths, Science, ICT

Teacher/Support:

Start date:

Review date:

IEP no.:

Targets:
1. To sit near the teacher/LSA.
2. To be able to distinguish between words ending in p/b/t/d.
3. To be able to spell c-v-c words ending in p/b/d/t.
4. To read to an adult on a daily basis – in addition to work in the literacy hour.

Strategies for use in class:
1. Always say x's name before asking a question.
2. Try to face x when speaking to him.
3. Try to keep background noise to a minimum whenever possible.
4. Give short instructions, have visual reminders whenever possible.
5. Make sure x always sits near the front for whole class situations.

Role of Parent(s)/Carer(s):
1. To hear x read at least 3 times per week.
2. To help with spellings.
3. To contact school whenever hearing is affected by colds, etc.

Success Criteria:
1. x sits near the teacher/LSA without being reminded.
2. To demonstrate 95% success on at least 3 separate occasions.
3. As above.
4. Reading diary that shows this has been accomplished.

Resources:
1. Various games including 'Thump the sound', 'Post boxes', etc.
2. Letter frames for c-v-c words and plastic letters.
3. A variety of workbooks.
4. Letter fans.
5. Reading buddies.
6. LSA for 10 minutes 3 times per week to do specific work on sound discrimination.
7. ALS group.

Agreed by:

SENCO:

Parent(s)/Carer(s):

Pupil:

Date:

Glue Ear

As many as four out of five children have at least one bout of glue ear before their fourth birthday. A substantial number experience regular, recurring symptoms throughout the primary years. These children will benefit from their teachers and parents knowing about the steps they can take to minimise the effects of glue ear.

What is glue ear?

Glue ear occurs when fluid collects in the middle ear space of one or both ears. This often happens after a cold or an infection in the ear or throat, when bacteria get into the middle ear and cause an inflammation of its lining. The Eustachian tubes can become blocked with mucus, making thing worse. The cells from the lining of the middle ear start to use up the remaining air, reducing the pressure in the middle ear space and allowing fluid to fill up the space. The fluid is often quite thin and runny but may become thicker, like glue, and prevent the ear-drum moving freely, resulting in temporary hearing loss.

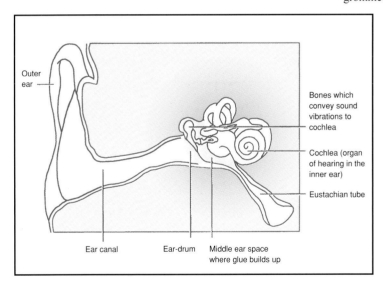

Outer ear

Bones which convey sound vibrations to cochlea

Cochlea (organ of hearing in the inner ear)

Eustachian tube

Ear canal   Ear-drum   Middle ear space where glue builds up

What are the signs of glue ear?

Children with glue ear experience differing degrees of hearing loss, from mild to severe, and their condition may change from day to day. Teachers and parents should watch out for the following indications:

- children who are inattentive, appearing to hear 'only when they want to'
- children who are talking more loudly than usual or talking less and becoming detached

- children turning up the sound control on TV, audio player or computer
- saying 'pardon' or 'what' more than usual
- failing to hear a sound which comes from outside their field of vision
- children experiencing discomfort or pain as a result of an infection in the ear
- children who are quiet and withdrawn as a result of poor hearing
- young children may become very tired by the end of the day because of the extra effort required to concentrate on what is being said

What can be done?

For about half the children who have glue ear, symptoms clear up naturally within three months; for others, a visit to the doctor may be necessary. If glue ear is a recurring problem, the child may be referred to an Ear, Nose and Throat specialist (ENT) and/or an audiologist. In severe cases, the specialist may advise putting in grommets. These are miniature ventilation tubes which keep the middle ear aired and healthy. Grommets improve hearing immediately and usually stay in place for between six months and a year. When they come out, the small hole in the ear-drum should heal quickly.

How can teachers help?

- attract the child's attention by calling his name – *before* asking a question or giving an instruction
- talk face to face when possible, sitting or bending to the same level for one-to-one exchange
- in a whole-class teaching situation, seat the child at the front where he can see your face clearly
- speak up but don't shout
- cut down background noise where possible
- keep instructions short and simple
- when you are sure about a child's hearing loss, explain to his classmates how they can help

(There are particular implications for the phonics element of the Literacy Hour; the teacher will need to ensure that the child is hearing an appropriate sound during sound-symbol work especially. It may be necessary to re-visit this sort of work once the glue ear has cleared up, perhaps with the help of a classroom assistant.)

For an information leaflet on glue ear, contact
Defeating Deafness (Hearing Research Trust)
330-332 Gray's Inn Rd, London WC1X 8EE
Tel: 020 7833 1733

Communication with the hearing impaired pupil

- Step forward 'out of the crowd' to make it easy for the child to focus on you.

- Speak clearly and at a moderate pace; do not shout. Avoid over-pronunciation or exaggeration.

- Look in the direction of the pupil.

- Do not stand with your back to the light.

- Avoid blocking his visual access to your face – either by hand movements or by holding a book in a way which obscures your face. It is harder for the child to communicate with a person who has a beard and/or wears glasses, as these can 'mask' the facial expression.

- Use 'natural' body language to enhance instructions and explanations.

- Make sure that lighting is adequate to allow the child to see facial expressions clearly.

- Give plenty of context clues when introducing a new subject – start with something which is familiar to the child.

- In a group or class discussion, control the pace and be prepared to repeat points for the child with hearing impairment.

- Short phrases and sentences are easier to understand than single words.

- Try to reduce the general noise within the classroom and seat the child away from traffic noise, or the hum of the OHP.

- Present one source of information at a time. It is difficult for a child with hearing loss to focus on what you are saying at the same time as looking at a book or watching what you are writing on the board.

- Phrase questions to the child carefully and always say his name beforehand.

- Obtain feedback from the child at regular intervals – without drawing too much attention to him.

Hearing Impairment

The term 'hearing Impairment' is a generic term used to describe all hearing loss. The two terms most used by teachers of the deaf to describe hearing impairment are the type and degree of loss.

Types of loss

The main types of hearing loss are:

Mon aural: hearing loss in one ear only. This condition is relatively easy to cope with in the classroom if the teacher is aware of the child's 'good side' and can position him appropriately.

Conductive loss: the mechanism by which sound waves reach the nerve endings in the cochlea is impeded. This can be caused by a build up of wax in the ear, or foreign objects in the outer ear canal. One of the most common forms of conductive loss is an excess of fluid in the middle ear and young children especially are prone to this condition. (See Glue Ear on page 23)

Sensory loss: caused by damage to the nerves. There are no medical or surgical procedures that can help restore hearing if the loss is sensory. In many cases, hearing aids are prescribed to maximise residual hearing. (Hearing aids must be prescribed by an ENT specialist) A Cochlea Implant may be offered to a child whose hearing loss is too profound for hearing aids to alleviate.

Mixed loss: a mixture of conductive and sensory loss, usually found in young children. The conductive element can be helped by medical and/or surgical procedures.

Degree of loss

Mild: the child hears nearly all speech, but may mishear if not looking directly at the speaker, or if acoustics in the classroom are poor. This condition can be very difficult to identify.

Moderate: the child will have great difficulty in hearing anyone speaking who is not very close by, without a hearing aid. He may well rely on lip-reading and visual cues to aid understanding, without realising it. The child's own voice will give few clues to his having a hearing loss, but if you listen carefully, you may notice that he misses word endings such as ss, sh and leave out indefinite and definite articles (e.g. *the, a*).

Severe: will not be able to cope without a hearing aid and even with one, the child needs to use visual clues such as lipreading and body language to gain information. The spoken voice may be comprehensible but the child is limited in the use of verbs and adjectives. Sentences may be shortened and sound somewhat 'telegraphic' in construction.

Profound: the child will probably use a hearing aid but will rely on visual cues and/or British Sign Language to communicate. The child's own voice may seem incomprehensible to those not used to it, but many youngsters achieve a high level of oral language. Radio aids are sometimes used with children who have severe or profound hearing loss. These use radio waves to transmit the speaker's voice to the listener and consists of two parts: a transmitter worn by the speaker (teacher) and a receiver worn by the child.

The majority of children with hearing impairment in mainstream schools will have mild to moderate hearing loss and use oral/aural methods as their main mode of communication.

Royal Institue for the Deaf (RNID)
19-23 Featherstone St, London EC1Y 8SL
Tel: 0808 808 0123

British Deaf Association (BDA)
1-3 Worship St, London ECZA 2AB

British Association of Teachers of the Deaf (BATOD)
The Orchard, Leven, North Humberside
HU17 5QA
www.batod.org.uk

Basic hearing aid circuit

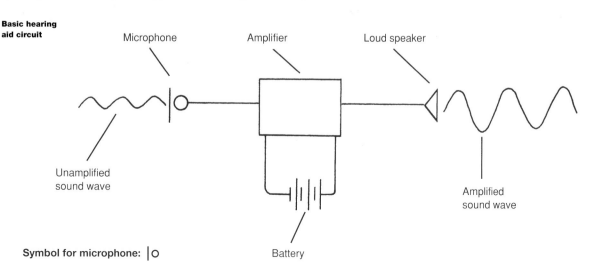

Microphone Amplifier Loud speaker

Unamplified sound wave

Amplified sound wave

Battery

Symbol for microphone: |o

INDIVIDUAL EDUCATION PLAN

Name:

Year: 2

Stage:

Area of concern: Language impairment

Strengths: Drawing

Teacher/Support: 5 hours LSA

Start date:

Review date:

IEP no.:

Role of Parent(s)/Carer(s):
1. To liaise with school regularly over language programme.
2. To hear x read at least 3 times per week.
3. To play games provided.

Targets:
1. To be able to answer 'when' and 'who' questions.
2. To use 'word trees' to learn new vocabulary for the Geography work.
3. To play ALS games in a group of 5/6.
4. To read 2 individual readers per week.

Strategies for use in class:
1. Ask another pupil a question first and then ask the same question of x to check understanding.
2. Ask x to repeat what they think they have to do for a task to check understanding.
3. Use x's ability to draw as an alternate form of recording.
4. Use some LSA time for individual reading sessions.
5. Present instructions in pictorial form if there are several.
6. Liaise with parents over the speech and language programme.
7. Make use of writing frames to aid writing.

Success Criteria:
1. Being able to answer 'when/who' questions about a variety of texts and in different lessons.
2. To be able to reproduce word trees for at least 6 new words from the Geography work.
3. Playing the ALS games observing the conventions of playing a game with a group, i.e. turn taking, talking, etc.
4. Evidence in the reading diary – this should include evidence of discussion work.

Resources:
1. Language programme provided by the Speech and Language therapist.
2. Picture cards for discussion.
3. Instruction templates – to add pictures.
4. ALS games.
5. 5 hours LSA time – one hour per day to include 20 minutes for language programme, 20 minutes individual reading sessions, 20 minutes ALS games with a group.
6. Writing frames.

Agreed by:

SENCO:

Parent(s)/Carer(s):

Pupil:

Date:

Language Impairment

Some children do not develop speech and language as expected. They may have difficulties with any or all aspects of speech and language, ranging from moving the muscles that control speech to the ability to understand or use language at all. The effects of language impairment can range from mild and transient to severe and long term. It is estimated that 6 in 100 children will have speech, language or communication difficulties at some stage and that 1 in 500 will experience severe, long-term difficulties. Most classroom teachers will have a child with some difficulties in their class.

What are the causes?

There is a range of causes and it is important to remember that language difficulties affect different aspects of the language system and can result in different patterns of performance. Some of those causes include:

- Genetics – language impairment can be inherited
- The environment – there is a link between disadvantage and poor language skills
- Injury – this can include brain injury
- Illness – such as stroke, Multiple Sclerosis or Motor Neurone Disease
- Hearing problems
- General learning difficulties
- A biological difficulty such as a cleft palate

What is language impairment?

There are different areas of language learning and, therefore, different forms of language impairment:

Speech apparatus – this includes the mouth, tongue, lips, nose, muscles and breathing. Any one, or all of these can be functioning incorrectly or inefficiently and lead to a language impairment. Some children will suffer from dysfluency or stammering.

Phonology – this refers to the sounds that make up the language. If a child has difficulty with phonology they use the wrong sounds.

Syntax or grammar – this is the way that words are put together in phrases or sentences. Some children cannot put the words together so that they can be understood.

Semantics – refers to the meaning of words and sentences. Children can find it difficult to remember the meaning of words.

Pragmatics – refers to how language is used in different situations and how feelings are conveyed.

Prosody (intonation and stress) – refers to the rhythm of the way we speak.

Within all of the above some children have difficulties with either receptive or expressive language and some with both.

Receptive language – understanding the meaning of what others say.

Expressive language – using language to communicate so that others understand what you say.

Education and participation in society depend on the ability to communicate. Some children have specific language difficulties but others have additional difficulties such as hearing problems or motor difficulties.

Aphasia/dysphasia – these two terms are now accepted to mean the same and refer to a disorder of language. The ability to understand and express words is affected. In turn this can affect the understanding of speech, reading, speaking, writing, gesture and/or signing, using numbers or doing calculations. Those who suffer often explain this as knowing what they want to say but being unable to remember the words. Aphasia can be either acquired or developmental.

What is the impact of language impairment?

Language impairment can be isolating and distressing. It can lead to a loss of confidence, lack of self-esteem and affect personal and social relationships. Also, it reduces opportunities in education. Research indicates that children with more complex language problems have a greater likelihood of experiencing behaviour problems. It can also affect concentration and memory. Children with speech and language impairments need to be taught the speech, language and social communication skills that other children learn naturally. The best results are gained where there is early intervention.

How can we help?

- Speech and language therapy – refer as soon as possible
- Regular speech and language sessions with either a teacher or trained assistant following a programme from the therapist
- Use signs and gestures
- Use pictures and/or symbols
- Both of the above can be used as teaching aids or as prompt cards
- Speak in short, simple sentences
- Give one instruction at a time
- Give a written list of instructions if appropriate
- Ask the child to repeat what they think they have to do, to check understanding
- Use circle time and social stories
- Teach word association skills for word finding difficulties
- Use games to encourage listening and social skills
- Have a 'word of the day/week' for the whole class
- Use individual reading sessions to talk about pictures, storyline or meanings as appropriate to the age of the child
- Teach the meanings of jokes, puns, etc.
- Be aware that misunderstanding can lead to possible behaviour and/or social problems

ICAN
4, Dyer's Buildings, Holborn, London EC1N 2QP
Tel: 0870 010 4066
www.afasic.org.uk
www.ican.org.uk
www.ukconnect.org
www.cafamily.org.uk

INDIVIDUAL EDUCATION PLAN

Name:

Year: 2

Stage:

Area of concern: Handwriting

Strengths: Keen to do well.

Teacher/Support:

Start date:

Review date:

IEP no.: 2

Targets:

1. To sit correctly at the table with paper tilted to the right.
2. To be able to use a pair of scissors to cut out accurately.
3. To form letters so that descenders are clear.

Strategies for use in class:

1. Make sure x is not sitting to the right of a right-handed child.
2. Encourage the use of Berol writing pen for ease of flow.
3. Encourage good posture at the table with feet on the floor.
4. Mark paper/book position on the table with tape until correct position established.
5. Ensure left-handed scissors are kept separately and clearly marked.
6. Have lots of practice work for letter formation.

Role of Parent(s)/Carer(s):

1. To encourage letter formation write in air, on margarine carton lids etc.
2. To play cutting out, making models, etc.

Success Criteria:

1. Demonstrating correct sitting position without being reminded.
2. The ability to cut out a variety of shapes accurately.
3. Letters written consistently in prose with clear descenders.

Resources:

1. Berol pens.
2. Brightly coloured masking tape to anchor/position paper
3. Left-handed scissors.
4. 'One-a-day' practice sheets, Teodorescu writing books.

Agreed by:

SENCO:

Parent(s)/Carer(s):

Pupil:

Date:

Left-handed writers

I t is estimated that around ten per cent of children are left handed. There are different levels of left-side-preference; one pupil may write and draw with his left hand, kick a football with his left foot and also be left-eye dominant, while another may be left handed but right footed and right eye dominant. Such a pupil may be described as cross-lateral and may be clumsy due to his left eye and right hand not co-ordinating very well.

Parents and teachers used to discourage children from using their left hand – to the extent of tying it behind their back, or making them sit on their left hand during lessons. Nowadays it is considered more sensible to allow children to develop right or left hand dominance naturally and do all that we can to alleviate any problems caused by being left handed in a mainly right-handed world.

In school, the activity likely to cause the most concern to left-handed children is writing. If you are right handed, take a few minutes to transfer your pen to the left hand and write a few sentences; you will find that it is much harder to push the pen across the page than it is to pull it, you can't easily see what you have written and your normal (undoubtedly correct) letter formation becomes much more tricky. There are ways however, of making life in the classroom easier for left-handers with just a little forethought.

How can we help?

Position
- Avoid the situation where a left-handed child has a right handed child next to her on her left: both youngsters will be competing for the same elbow room.
- Ensure a good writing posture; this calls for furniture of the correct size so that the child can put both feet on the floor and place his arms comfortably on the table; it can help left-handed writers to raise their seat slightly, giving them a better view of their writing. A sloping surface sometimes helps too.
- The position of the paper can make a big difference to ease of writing; tilt to the right for a left-handed writer.

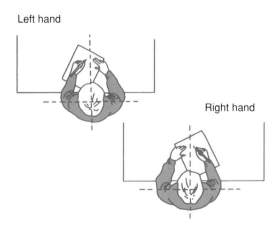

Left hand

Right hand

Modelling writing
Demonstrate letter formation with your left hand for left-handed writers.

Pencil grip
- Children develop all sorts of penholds, though one of the best ways to hold a pencil, allowing for easy, controlled movement, is the tripod grip. The most important consideration is that the penhold is relaxed and comfortable; there is no right or wrong way and once a penhold is established, it is very difficult to change. If the child grips too tightly, presses very hard on the paper or twists her hand awkwardly, the act of writing can become very uncomfortable and difficult to sustain.

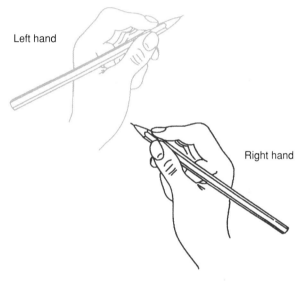

Left hand

Right hand

Materials
- The choice of paper and pen/pencil can make a huge difference. Try writing neatly with a stub of wax crayon on sugar paper! There is a huge range of pens and pencils from which to choose and it is worth encouraging a left-handed child in particular, to experiment.
- For those who have difficulty in holding a writing implement comfortably, various types of grip are available which can be attached to the pen or pencil and may be of help.
(Remember to provide left-handed scissors for cutting out.)

Practice
- A left-handed writer may need to practise more in the early stages; put together a selection of handwriting activities which he can practice at home and explain to parents or carers how they can help and encourage.

Everything Left-handed
5, Charles St, Worcester WR1 2AQ
Tel: 01905 25798

INDIVIDUAL EDUCATION PLAN

Name:

Year: 7

Stage:

Area of concern: Literacy difficulties

Strengths: Enjoys reading and having books read to him

Teacher/Support: LSA to support in English lessons

Start date:

Review date:

IEP no.:

Role of Parent(s)/Carer(s):
1. Regular reading; Monday, Wednesday, Thursday after tea for fifteen minutes – *X* reading to you, or you reading to him. Talk about the stories, 'Which bit did you like best? What would you do if...?'
2. Writing the shopping list on Friday night – help him out with spellings.

Targets:
1. To answer questions about a text:
   a. verbally
   b. in multiple choice exercises
   c. in short written sentences.
2. To practise reading every day and complete three books from the 'blue box' every week.
3. To improve spelling accuracy.
4. To write legibly and more quickly.

Strategies for use in class:
1. Give *x* frequent opportunities to follow text as you read out loud.
2. Check his understanding by questioning.
3. Encourage him to use his key word dictionary and provide a word wall of subject-specific vocabulary. Use the Look-Cover-Write-Check method for learning spellings.
4. Give praise for correct spellings.
5. Specify how much writing *x* should complete in a lesson (it requires a huge effort for him to write 50 words which are legible) and insist that it is legible.
6. Provide a pen if he has lost/forgotten his own.
7. Make use of alternative methods of recording where appropriate: diagram, poster, audio recording, word processing.

Success Criteria:
1. To complete the first three units of work in the scheme, with 80% accuracy.
2. To read three books each week with Mrs Smith, during the lunch-time study session.
3. To spell correctly 100 key words.
4. To finish pieces of writing in subject lessons and in a legible hand.

Resources:
1. Student books from the scheme.
2. Reading books from the blue box (reading age 7-8).
3. 'Talking books' on loan to take home.
4. Handwriting practice sheets.
5. Key words dictionary and LCWC book.

Agreed by:

SENCO:

Parent(s)/Carer(s):

Pupil:

Date:

Moderate Learning Difficulties
(MLD)

The largest group of children and young adults with special educational needs are those defined as having Moderate Learning Difficulties, or Global Learning Difficulties (GLD). These are pupils with general developmental delay. They are increasingly placed in mainstream schools and may constitute as much as twenty per cent of any school population. They may once have been referred to as 'slow learners' or 'remedials' and for the most part, will be found in the 'bottom sets' in school. These pupils do not find learning easy and often experience very little success in school. Their self esteem can plummet, especially in secondary school and this may result in unacceptable behaviour as they search for a way of avoiding failure, putting on a show of bravado and impressing their peers.

The main characteristics are:

- Difficulties with reading and writing, and comprehension
- Poor understanding of basic mathematical concepts
- Immature social and emotional skills
- Limited communication skills
- Short attention span
- Under-developed co-ordination skills
- Lack of logical reasoning
- Inability to generalise what they learn and apply it to other situations

They may have problems with:

- Understanding what is required of them
- Remembering what has been taught (short term and long term)
- Acquiring sequencing skills
- Dyspraxia ('clumsiness')
- Organising themselves
- Auditory/visual memory

They may also have a variety of syndromes and/or medical conditions.

How can we help?

Children with moderate learning difficulties are often very conscious that they are 'lagging behind'. Everything possible should be done to enhance their self-esteem and persuade them that they can learn, albeit with a great deal of effort.

- Find out as much about the child as possible. Use SATs scores, reading age and any diagnostic data, to help you ascertain his strengths and weaknesses.
- Use your own observation skills to build up a profile of the child, noticing how he responds to different teaching styles

- Make sure that the learning objectives are realistic for every lesson, and that he can experience some success
- Break down any new task into small steps and build in lots of opportunities for reinforcement
- Be prepared to allow him extra time to finish a task
- Check understanding at every stage
- Establish a supportive relationship
- Use appropriate praise and encouragement: catch him being good as well as complimenting him for finishing work and trying hard
- Liaise with the SENCo who will be able to suggest strategies and resources: differentiated texts, word banks, language master, writing frames, ICT software (and modified hardware)

It may be necessary to prepare individual work sometimes for a pupil or a small group; enlarging the print and shortening a passage is a simple process which can make an immediate difference to the accessibility of text. Make an overhead transparency of the text and project this while you read it out, perhaps several times, then let pupils practice together before having a go on their own. Children who struggle with reading need to have frequent practice in every subject of the curriculum. Provide writing frames or activity sheets which minimise the amount of writing required; if the child is involved in a science experiment, you want him to observe and record what happens, not spend forty minutes trying to draw a bunsen burner.

- Establish a routine within the lesson so that pupils know what to expect and most important, what is expected of them
- Keep tasks short and build in variety
- Establish what the child already knows about a topic; be prepared to go back to the point where he is on firm ground
- Repeat information in different ways
- Use careful questioning to ensure the pupil's participation and check his understanding
- Short, daily practice of key skills like telling the time, multiplication tables and spellings is more effective than longer sessions
- Show the child what to do as well as talking about it: give concrete examples, provide a model

Learning assistants

Learning assistants can be an invaluable asset to teachers. The objectives of the lesson and any differentiation required for MLD pupils to achieve, should be discussed between teacher and LSA so that there is adequate preparation and a shared understanding of goals. Sometimes, pupils can come to depend on their LSA for propping them up. It is important to encourage independence and establish a relationship which is supportive without being cosseting.

INDIVIDUAL EDUCATION PLAN

Name:

Year:

Stage:

Area of concern: Semantic Pragmatic Disorder

Strengths: Rote memory

Teacher/Support:

Start date:

Review date:

IEP no.: 2

Targets:

1. To use a task board each session.
2. To be able to take part in a game with two other children.
3. To organise the lunch boxes.
4. To learn to put a hand up and wait for help when needed.

Strategies for use in class:

1. Make instructions explicit.
2. Prepare for any changes to routine.
3. Ask him to repeat what he has to do to check for meaning.
4. Model how to organise lunch boxes, including how to talk to people.
5. Use cards to reinforce the hands up rule.
6. During literacy and numeracy ask straightforward questions and allow time to answer.
7. Build in work on explaining jokes.
8. Make good use of computer programs.

Role of Parent(s)/Carer(s):

1. Regular contact with class teacher.
2. To play literacy and numeracy games at home.
3. To share stories.

Success Criteria:

1. Being able to follow the task board without help.
2. Taking part on at least five different occasions.
3. Showing that they have learnt the appropriate language and can organise appropriately.
4. No longer getting out of seat to fetch an adult.

Resources:

1. Task board and stickers.
2. LSA for five hours per week – to include 10 minutes per day on language work.
3. Literacy and numeracy games – from ALS pack.
4. Resources provided by Speech and Language Therapist.
5. Circle time/social stories resources.

Agreed by:

SENCO:

Parent(s)/Carer(s):

Pupil:

Date:

Semantic Pragmatic
Disorder

Semantic Pragmatic Disorder is a communication disorder, (semantic = the meanings of words and sentences, pragmatic = making language work in context). Children with SPD have difficulty in processing all the information from a situation and often do not respond appropriately.

The disorder relates to autism in that it involves difficulties in the same three areas: socialising, language and imagination (The Triad).

Switched off

Most children absorb information easily, processing and analysing it, discarding what is unimportant or uninteresting and storing the rest. They are able to build up a memory bank of words and their meanings, including those which relate to concepts such as time and personal feelings, which may not have a visual reference. They use this data together with their past experience of the world, to predict how other people will react to certain things, to understand their intentions and forecast what might happen next.

A child with Semantic Pragmatic Disorder has an imperfect 'information processing' system and will have problems in knowing what to say, sometimes appearing rude or outspoken, and not realising that the listener has 'had enough'. He may talk at great length about something which interests him, but not realise that the listener has 'switched off'.

Characteristics:

- speaks fluently, sometimes in a very grown-up way, but on his own terms

- inappropriate eye-contact/facial expression

- difficulty in giving specific information

- problems with abstract concepts – (imagine, guess, next week)

- can appear rude, arrogant, gauche

- easily distracted

- motor skills problems

- over-sensitive to certain noises etc.

In school, these children need:

- straightforward, specific and unambiguous instructions, e.g. 'put the pencils in the blue box', not 'tidy up'

- practical, hands-on tasks

- a quiet, orderly working environment

- predictability in the classroom routine – give clear signals for any changes

- time to reply when asked a question

- specific activities to help with socialising

- clear rules on how to behave

- regular reminders, supported by visual/written information (e.g. a task board)

- adults to interpret what the child 'means' rather than accept what he actually says when he doesn't make sense

- explanations about sarcasm, metaphors, jokes – don't take for granted that he understands

- a teacher to double-check their understanding

- to be taught the meanings of idiomatic expressions and appropriate language for different situations

- constant encouragement and praise

National Autistic Society
www.nas.org.uk
email: nas@mailbox.ulcc.ac.uk

INDIVIDUAL EDUCATION PLAN

Name:

Year: 6

Stage:

Area of concern: Tourettes Syndrome

Strengths: ICT skills

Teacher/Support: 5 hours SSA

Start date:

Review date:

IEP no.:

Targets:
1. To be able to remove self from room when necessary.
2. To attend computer club at lunch times (to relieve stress of unstructured times).
3. To walk away and report any incidents of teasing (rather than retaliation).

Strategies for use in class:
1. A small card that will be displayed on the table to indicate a need to leave.
2. Encouraging reminders to the whole class of times for computer club.
3. *x* has agreed that Tourette's Syndrome can be used as a discussion for PSHE alongside other conditions.
4. Allow *x* to sit at the back of the class where he feels comfortable.
5. If you notice the tics becoming more regular use the card to indicate time out is needed.
6. Make regular use of the computer to aid written tasks and concentration.
7. Encourage peer mentoring.

Role of Parent(s)/Carer(s):
1. To keep staff informed.
2. To help with homework

Success Criteria:
1. Having demonstrated the ability to do this appropriately on five separate occasions.
2. Attendance on a regular basis of twice a week as agreed.
3. No incidences of fights because of teasing.

Resources:
1. A copy of *x*'s indication card will be available in the teacher's desk in all rooms.
2. Further information on Tourette's Syndrome available in the staff room in *Special Children* folder.
3. A space has been made available in the library for use if needed.
4. A separate room has been organised for *x* to take his SATs.
5. Parents have provided a full description of how TS affects *x* and the signs to look for.

Agreed by:

SENCO:

Parent(s)/Carer(s):

Pupil:

Date:

Tourette's Syndrome

Tourette's Syndrome is one of a number of *tic* disorders. It is characterised by many varied, frequently changing *tics*. Current research indicates that it is an inability to regulate dopamine which is a neuro-transmitter, resulting in the impaired action of various receptor sites. It is a neurobiological disorder that is genetically inherited. It can be triggered by a streptococcal infection but it is not the infection itself that causes the trigger but the body's antibodies. It is estimated that 3% of the population may have Tourette's Syndrome with a ratio of 4:1 males to females.

What is a tic?

A tic is an involuntary rapid or sudden movement or sound that is repeated over and over again. A tic can start as blinking or sniffing or can progress to be as extreme as coprolalia, copropraxia, echolalia or echopraxia.

Coprolalia – the repetition of obscene words.
Copropraxia – the repetition of obscene gestures.
Echolalia – the repetition of what you last heard.
Echopraxia – imitating the actions you saw.

It must be stressed that the majority of children have TS in the mild form and are probably undiagnosed. The extreme forms mentioned above are only found in a minority but tend to hit the headlines!

Tics often disappear during sleep though not always. They are usually worse during times of stress and/or excitement and when the child is extremely tired. It is interesting for schools to note that they can subside during periods of extreme concentration such as at a computer or when engaged in a favourite activity.

People who suffer from tics say that they are often aware when they are going to occur, but that it is like a sneeze in that they can do nothing about it. Some people learn to suppress their tics for a while but that will mean they return with a vengeance once the person relaxes.

Transient tics – 1 in 5 children will have a tic at some time but these are mainly transient and only last a few weeks or months. They may have several episodes over several years and they may change from one to another such as from sniffing to hair twirling.

Chronic tic disorder – this is where the tics do not change and will remain unchanged for years. A person may have several chronic tics.

Treatment

This is often not necessary and an explanation may be all that is needed to help the individual understand. If the tics are causing problems then medication can be prescribed but there is a period of trial until identifying which provides the optimum benefit.

Types of Tourette's Syndrome:

1. Pure Tourette's Syndrome – often goes undiagnosed and is not associated with other conditions.
2. Full blown TS – Will include the extremes such as coprolalia and/or copropraxia.
3. TS Plus – Where associated conditions are present.

Pure TS often causes no behavioural or educational problems but it is the associated disorders that lead to difficulties.

Associated Disorders:

● Attention Deficit Hyperactivity Disorder (ADHD)
● Obsessive Compulsive Disorder (OCD)
● Oppositional Defiant Disorder (ODD)
● Self-injurious behaviour
● Outbursts of aggression
● Depression
● Fine motor control problems
● Organisational problems
● Reading comprehension difficulties

Children with TS follow the normal curve of distribution of intelligence, however, they are more likely to experience learning difficulties than the general population. The condition is often misunderstood and everyone associated with the child needs a knowledge and understanding of how it affects the individual child.

How can we help?

● Talk to the parents (and child if appropriate)
● Prevent teasing at all costs
● Allow extra time to prevent stress
● Provide time-out for when tics become disruptive
● Have a discrete sign so that the individual can leave to release tics in private
● Encourage the student to monitor themselves so they know when they need a break
● Allow to sit at the back to prevent staring
● Provide a separate room for exams
● Be flexible – if reading is affected by eye/neck tics provide an alternative
● If loud vocal tics – allow to miss large group, quiet times such as assembly
● Make use of a computer to cut down on handwriting
● Use multi-sensory strategies, especially practical activities
● Pair with a mentor if the tics would make an activity unsafe, such as an experiment
● If it is a touching tic allow for a buffer zone but be careful not to isolate
● Plan for times of excitement such as birthdays, trips, etc.
● A library carrel or private area may help
● If tics are exhausting break work into smaller chunks
● Be watchful of depression
● Do NOT punish a tic!

Safety considerations

- Use textured flooring where possible to differentiate between areas

- Floor coverings should be checked regularly for holes: check for slippery surfaces and crumbling steps outside

- Paint white strips on steps, stairs and hand rails

- Stick transfers or pictures on large expanses of plain glass

- Keep classroom floors free of clutter such as schoolbags, coats and electric cables; make sure that corridors are 'clearways'

- Avoid having objects hanging at head height – plants, mobiles, 'washing lines for paintings', or make sure the child knows exactly where the 'obstacles' are

- Beware of windows at head height which open out into a thoroughfare, or on to the playground

- Have good, consistent lighting around the school

- Make sure that other pupils understand how they can help the child with visual impairment, for example by refraining from swinging backwards on their chairs, or suddenly pushing back their chair to get up

- Encourage orderly movement around the school, a 'keep to the left' system and no running

- Teach pupils to take special care with sharp objects such as scissors

Safety considerations for schools with pupils who have impaired vision

Visual Impairment

The vast majority of children with sight problems are educated in mainstream schools where, given appropriate support, they can thrive. In some cases however, children's problems are not recognised or sufficiently understood and it is in these cases that problems tend to arise.

Teachers and learning assistants are well-placed to carefully observe children and take note of any behaviour which indicates a sight problem; further investigation by a GP or optician should always be recommended to parents and carers where there is a concern.

What to look out for

- Inflamed, weepy, cloudy or bloodshot eyes
- Squints and eyes that do not seem to be aligned and working together
- Rapid, involuntary eye movements
- Continual blinking, rubbing or screwing-up of eyes
- Discomfort in bright light
- The child holding his head in an awkward position or holding his book at an unusual angle/distance
- Frequent headaches or dizziness
- Clumsiness, bumping into furniture etc
- Poor balance
- Failure to respond appropriately to questions, commands or gestures unless addressed directly by name; inappropriate response to non-verbal communication
- Difficulty in copying form the board, poor presentation skills, confusion between similarly shaped letters/words

Symptoms such as these may result in the child being unable to engage with the learning task in hand and in his becoming 'switched off'.

How can we help?

- If the child has glasses, encourage him to wear them and to keep them clean
- Find out from the specialist VI teacher, as much as you can about the child's condition and the implications for classroom work
- Always give clear instructions and descriptions – the child may mis-read gestures and facial expressions
- Use the child's name to get his attention – looking at him may not be enough
- Allow him to sit at the front of the class or near to the board, big book, television or OHP screen. Provide him with his own copy of the text where possible
- Allow extra time for finishing tasks

- Always provide him with a book of his own rather than expecting him to share
- Do not stand with your back to the window; this creates silhouetting and makes it harder for the child to see you
- Make sure that there is good lighting in work areas, with no glare. Some children are photophobic (sensitive to light), and may be more comfortable in a shaded area of the room
- The pupil with impaired vision will tire more quickly than his peers – short tasks are preferable to long, sustained sessions
- Draw the child's attention to displays – otherwise they may go unnoticed
- Encourage personal tidiness and identify some personal space for the VI child. Pegs and lockers should be at the end of rows and not shared
- Find out about specialist equipment that can enable the child to be more independent in practical lessons, (e.g. talking scales)

All resource material should be of good quality and well-spaced:

- Avoid cluttering the pages of worksheets with illustrations and ornate script.
- Enlarge the text to

16 point or **18 point**

where possible.
- Avoid *italic* or *ornate* scripts.
- Remember that lower case script is easier to read than CAPITAL LETTERS, because it has ascenders and descenders to give it a more distinctive shape.
- Shorter lines of text are easier to follow, and an unjustified right hand margin helps the reader.
- Use paper with a matt surface rather than a glossy surface which may create glare.

The child with more severely impaired vision may need specialised equipment and there is a range of magnifying equipment which your VI service will be able to advise on.

RNIB (Royal National institute for the Blind)
224, Great Portland Street,
London W1W 5AA
Tel: 020 7388 1266
www.rnib.org.uk

Asthma

An ever-increasing number of children are affected by asthma, some experts say as many as one in seven children in the UK are affected by asthma, wheeze or chronic cough. The causes of this increase are not entirely clear. Exposure to traffic-related pollution has popularly been blamed as a major cause, and it is clear that asthma sufferers are more likely to experience an attack on polluted days. There is no firm evidence, however, to show that people who live in more polluted areas are necessarily more prone to be asthma sufferers in the first place. A wide range of other factors are also important. Exposure to tobacco smoke and house dust mite are certainly amongst the most serious risk factors; others include damp and mould, food additives, pollen and spores, and fur and feathers. Whatever the causes, asthma can be both a discomforting and a debilitating disease.

What is Asthma?

Asthma is a common disease in which the circular smooth muscles of the branching air tubes of the lungs, the bronchi, are liable to go into spasm so that the bronchi are narrowed and the passage of air

muscle   mucus   muscles   lining
                       tighten   swells

airway   airway   extra
                 narrows   mucus

impeded. It is often easier to breathe in than out and the lungs become inflated and cannot easily be emptied. A wheeze on breathing out is a regular feature of an asthma attack. The commonest kind is allergic asthma, but asthma can also be induced by infection, emotion, occupation and exertion.

Narrowing of the tubes carrying air into lungs, as a result of tightening of the muscles in their walls, is called 'Bronchospasm'. While bronchospasm is the main feature of asthma, it also occurs in other allergic conditions and other lung diseases, such as emphysema and chronic bronchitis. The result of bronchospasm is

a restriction in the flow of air. This is often worse on breathing out than breathing in and there may be severe wheezing and a persistently inflated chest. It also causes coughing. Sometimes bronchospasm is so severe as to endanger life. Commonly it leads to an inadequate supply of oxygen to the tissues and the skin may appear blue, (Cyanosis).

An asthma attack can last for a few minutes or several hours, but sufferers learn to recognise the signs of the condition worsening and what to do to alleviate it. Asthma is treated with two main types of medicine, called **relievers** and **preventers**. Each medicine works in a different way, but both need to be breathed in deeply to reach the lungs. They come in small packs called inhalers or puffers.

Reliever medicines relieve the symptoms of asthma straight away by relaxing the muscles around the airways so that they open wider and make breathing easier. The medicine does not treat the inflammation in the airway itself. Reliever inhalers are usually blue and children must have access to their inhaler at all times.

Preventer medicines calm the inflamed airways and stop them being irritated so easily. This helps to calm the asthma and reduces the risk of an attack. The effect of the medicine builds up over time so it has to be taken every day

How can we help?

There are no learning difficulties associated with asthma and all but the most severely affected children are able to cope in mainstream schools. It is important however, that all staff know when a child has the condition and are familiar with the procedure to be followed if he has an attack. There are five basic rules:

- Stay calm – anxiety can aggravate the attack. Reassure the child, but don't put your arm round him
- Find the child's reliever inhaler and make sure he uses it correctly
- Encourage him to sit upright and lean forwards
- Loosen tight clothing and offer a drink of water
- Call medical help if the medication fails to relieve the attack in five to ten minutes – the child should continue to use his reliever inhaler every few minutes until the doctor or ambulance arrives

Asthma attacks are often brought on by exercise, especially in cold, dry weather; this can often be prevented by the use of an inhaler before a PE lesson and by 'warming-up' gradually. Care should be taken to ensure that a child does not use his asthma as an excuse to avoid P.E. However, regular exercise, especially swimming, is beneficial. Always check with parents or carers for guidance on this matter.

National Asthma Campaign,
Providence House, Providence Place,
Islington London N1 ONT
Tel: 020 7226 2260
www.asthma.org.uk

Brittle Bones

Brittle Bones is a genetic disorder known medically as *Osteogenesis Imperfecta* (OI). Brittle Bones actually refers to a range of conditions resulting from abnormalities in the protein structure of the bones that leads to the bones breaking more easily. It is **not** caused by a lack of calcium. The milder forms are usually inherited but for others the genetic mutation happens 'out of the blue'. Because the genetic defect is dominant, a carrier has a 50% chance of passing on the condition to his/her children. About 1 in 20,000 babies are born with Brittle Bones each year. There is no cure at present but work on treatment is progressing.

Some children are born with fractures; some suffer them soon after birth and others when they first start to walk. Children can suffer anything from 10 to 100 or more fractures during childhood. There is no general indication of how frequently a child will suffer from fractures and some are more vulnerable than others. Each fracture has to be managed individually as it occurs. Sometimes children go through a 'bad spell' when they have several breaks one after another and then they can go years without one. There is evidence to show that adolescents do not fracture as frequently as younger children. Fractures can be caused by perfectly normal behaviour such as closing a door or turning over in bed and whereas schools should make every effort to ensure the safety of the child it should not be held responsible for any breaks that occur at school.

What are the characteristics?

Some children are of normal stature and simply more fragile whereas others who are more severely affected can be of short stature and unable to walk. Children with the severe type may have spent much of their early life lying on their back in plaster and may have missed out on a range of experiences. This in turn can affect confidence and learning. There may be problems with gross motor skills and children may take longer to learn to walk or sit. Often children have lax joints and loose muscles that lead to difficulties with fine motor skills. Children with Brittle Bones are often left-handed because they experience fewer breaks with that arm. They may hold their pen or pencil with an unconventional grip and find it difficult to write for long periods. Most, given the right support, can lead active lives but many may need to use sticks, crutches or wheelchairs for support and safety. PE and Games are not generally recommended but swimming and non-weight bearing exercise are beneficial. More unusual characteristics include a triangular shaped face, progressive limb deformities, chronic bone pain and hearing difficulties. Those who are most severely affected often have respiratory problems because of under-developed lungs.

The vast majority of children are of normal intelligence and have no needs other than physical ones. However, it is important to bear in mind the emotional needs of a child growing up with a condition that they feel may restrict their lives. There is a balance to be found between being over protective and allowing the freedom to take risks. Education is important as, given the right opportunities, children with the condition can lead independent lives.

How can we help?

- Talk to parents and the child
- Get the advice of an Occupational Therapist – they will be able to help on simple adaptations and/or specialist equipment that may need to be made at each stage of education
- Make use of specially adapted keyboards or voice activated packages for computers if finger movement is restricted
- For handwriting problems consider:
  A sloping desk
  Different sizes/shapes of pen
  Seating arrangements
  Providing handouts/copies of notes
  Dictaphone
- Make sure everyone is aware and knows what to do in the event of a break
- With permission from the child and his/her parents inform the child's peers through PSHE
- Be flexible with arrangements for the playground and movement in school – allowing the child to leave a couple of minutes before or after everyone else should suffice
- Use a buddy system to help at times such as lunch
- **Expect high academic standards**
- Provide pastoral support – this is particularly important as the child gets older
- Ensure effective liaison between school and hospital and/or home tuition when needed
- Plan ahead for transfers
- Plan for time missed because of breaks
- Encourage participation in out-of-school activities – depending on the severity of their condition they may feel socially isolated
- Use a small cue card for the child to call for help – they are often reluctant to do so because they do not like to feel any more different than they are already

It is important to try to treat a child with Brittle Bones as normally as possible to ensure a healthy emotional development that will lead to independence.

www.brittlebone.org

Diabetes

Diabetes is a health condition that affects about 1.4 million people in the United Kingdom and it is estimated that another 1 million have the condition but don't know. About 1 in every 700 school children has the condition and both sexes are equally affected. It is a common condition in which the amount of glucose (sugar) in the blood is too high because the body's method of converting that glucose into energy is not working. The hormone insulin made by the pancreas normally controls it. It is important to remember that treatment is effective.

Types of Diabetes

There are two main types of diabetes and over three-quarters of those affected have Type 2.

● Type 1
This occurs when there is a severe lack of insulin because the cells in the pancreas have been destroyed. It usually appears in people under forty and often in childhood. Symptoms develop quickly and are obvious. These children are treated with insulin injections, which are vital to keep them alive, and through a carefully managed diet. Most children will have two injections a day, usually before breakfast and before an evening meal. However, a few may also need a lunchtime injection.

● Type 2
This is the type commonly found in the over-forties. It occurs when the pancreas cannot produce enough insulin for the needs of the body. Diet alone, diet and tablets or diet and injections, depending on the severity of need, can treat this type. It develops slowly and the symptoms are less severe. It often goes unnoticed because the symptoms are put down to getting older and over-work.

What are the symptoms?
- Increased thirst
- Going to the loo a lot
- Extreme tiredness
- Weight loss
- Genital itching
- Blurred vision

Adverse reactions

If the blood sugar becomes too low a person may develop **hypoglycaemia** and can become unconscious.
If the blood sugar is too high they may develop **hyperglycaemia**. It is the first of these two that is more likely to occur in school.

The causes:
- A missed snack – timing of food is important and some children may need to eat in lessons
- Extra exercise – it is important to encourage regular exercise but all staff must be aware that excessive exercise could lead to an episode if diet is not controlled
- Too much insulin
- Extremes of weather

The symptoms:
It is really important that everyone who comes into contact with the child is aware of these symptoms!

- Hunger
- Sweating
- Drowsiness
- Pallor
- Glazed eyes
- Shaking
- Mood change – especially aggression
- Lack of concentration

N.B. The parents and the child themselves will be able to tell you about their symptoms.

How to treat:
Give fast-acting sugar to raise blood glucose levels:

- Lucozade or other sugary drink – NOT diet varieties
- Mini chocolate bar
- Fresh fruit juice
- Glucose tablets
- Jam/honey – if the child is too confused to help himself or herself try rubbing jam or honey in the inside of the cheek

ALWAYS try to keep something for an emergency in the teacher's desk and in the child's pocket.
WHEN a child recovers from an episode they will need some slower-acting starchy food such as a sandwich. They may feel nauseous, tired and/or have a headache.
In the unlikely event that the child loses consciousness put them into the recovery position and call an ambulance.

Points to remember:
- Allow the child to visit the toilet regularly
- A younger child may need help with the timing of their food
- You may have to allow them to be first in the dinner queue
- Adolescents may rebel against the strict regime and may need some counselling
- ALL staff should know the symptoms to look for and how to react
- Regular exercise helps cut down on serious health problems later

Diabetes UK   www.diabetes.org.uk/
Careline: 020 7636 6112 Monday–Friday (9–5)

Epilepsy

Epilepsy is the second most common neurological disorder after migraine. It affects one in about every 130 people in the UK and 75% of them will have their first seizure before the age of 20. Most teachers will have at least one child with epilepsy in their class at some time in their career.

What is epilepsy?

The cause of epilepsy is a temporary change in the way brain cells work. An upset in brain chemistry means messages get scrambled and that causes neurons to fire off faster than usual. This 'electrical storm' interferes with normal functioning and triggers a seizure. There are forty different types of seizure caused by different chemical processes, sited in different areas of the brain.

Types of seizure

There are two main types of seizure; a *partial seizure* occurs when a specific part of the brain is affected and the nature of such fits depends upon the area of brain involved. The child will not pass out but consciousness will be affected. With a *generalised seizure* a large part of the brain is affected. Fits vary from major convulsive episodes, with jerking of limbs and unconsciousness, to momentary lapses of consciousness and fluttering eyelids.

However, two people who have the same type of seizure may have dramatically different experiences. They can vary from 'absence seizures' where the child may appear to be daydreaming to full 'tonic' seizures, sometimes referred to as *'grand-mal'*.

Treatment

The standard treatment is to give drugs that regulate the chemical processes in the brain and allow most children the chance to lead a 'normal' life. All the drugs aim to prevent rather than treat seizures, which is why those affected must take the same dose every day. All the drugs can cause side effects and it is important to monitor and change the drugs being used until the one that best suits an individual is found. If a child is drowsy or over-active it is vital to tell parents as this may be a sign that the medication needs adjusting.

Possible side effects of the drugs include: dizziness, headaches, nausea, tiredness, poor memory, slow reaction times and impaired motor control.

With adequate supervision there is no activity that needs to be barred but if a child has a history of frequent or unpredictable seizures it is probably wise to avoid climbing the wall bars! Swimming should be encouraged but make sure that a 'buddy' system is set up first.

What can trigger a seizure?

Most seizures strike completely out of the blue but certain factors can act as a trigger:
- Stress
- Patterns of light – many people believe that watching TV or playing video games can trigger a seizure. This is true in a few people who are photosensitive (sensitive to flickering light), though it is far less common than most people imagine. In fact only about five per cent of people with epilepsy are affected in this way
- Lack of sleep – too many late nights can trigger seizures
- Illness – a high temperature (fever) can bring on seizures
- Hormones – for some girls, seizures may be linked to their menstrual cycle
- Food – some people with epilepsy claim that certain foods trigger seizures. Apart from some severe types of childhood epilepsy however, there is no evidence to suggest that what you eat can bring on seizures. Skipping meals and a poor diet may be a factor

How to deal with a seizure

- Cushion the head with something soft
- DO NOT put anything in the mouth or between the teeth
- DO NOT give anything to drink until the seizure finishes
- Loosen tight clothing around the neck
- As soon as possible, or when movements subside, put the child in a semi-prone position to aid breathing
- Wipe away saliva
- KEEP CALM – REASSURE the child, especially in that confused period immediately following a seizure
- If incontinence occurs cover with a blanket
- There is no need for an ambulance UNLESS the seizure lasts for more than five minutes OR the child has a series of seizures without properly regaining consciousness between them
- Provide a place to rest
- Always inform parents when a seizure has occurred

Some general hints

- Talk to parents
- ALL staff in school must know what to do
- Allow for catching up missed work
- Be alert and prevent teasing. Explain to other children.
- Respond calmly – remember other children may be frightened
- Be alert for the 'daydreamer' – 30 to 40 absences per day can have a devastating effect on education
- Ensure that school records have full details of medication, type of seizure, etc. in case of an emergency

(See checklist over page.)

British Epilepsy Association:
www.epilepsy.org.uk
National Society for Epilepsy:
www.epilepsynse.org.uk

Seizure checklist

When a pupil has a seizure...

- Do not try to hold him down or stop him moving about

- Put something soft under his head and loosen collar and tie

- Move any furniture or anything with sharp edges so that he won't hurt himself

- Do not try to put anything in his mouth or make him drink anything

- Wait quietly with him until he knows where he is and what has happened

- Ask him if he wants to have a rest before going back to lessons

- Do not ring for an ambulance unless he has hurt himself or his seizure lasts longer than a few minutes

- Explain to his classmates what has happened and how they can help

- Help him to catch up with any work he has missed in class

- Let his parents know

Muscular Dystrophy
(MD)

Muscular dystrophy is a general term used to describe a group of about 20 types of genetic disorders that involve muscle weakness. It is caused by a fault on a particular gene that leads to damaged muscle fibres. Duchenne's Muscular Dystrophy is the most common childhood dystrophy and affects only males, but other types affect both sexes. Whilst some individuals can remain fairly stable for a time it is a progressive condition in which the muscles become weaker and weaker. The severity of the condition varies from one person to the next and life expectancy also varies a great deal.

Congenital Muscular Dystrophy (CMD)

The symptoms of CMD usually show from birth or within the first six months. These are:

● Hypotonia (floppiness)
● Poor head control
● Delayed motor milestones such as crawling and walking
● Tightness in the ankles, hips, knees and elbows
● Sometimes, dislocated hips

There are 3 main types of CMD:

1. Dystrophy – this is solely muscle weakness but all muscles are affected
2. Muscle weakness plus learning difficulties
3. Muscle weakness, learning difficulties and abnormalities of the eye

The learning difficulties that occur with types 2 and 3 cover the full spectrum, from subtle to severe. The pattern of inheritance is known as 'autosomal recessive', that means both parents are carriers and have a one in four chance of passing on the condition. It is estimated that 1 in 50,000 have CMD.

There is no cure but there are ways of alleviating the symptoms through therapy. Physiotherapy and Occupational Therapy (OT) services will be able to assist in school. A child with CMD can remain fairly stable but if the condition rapidly progresses it can lead to respiratory failure.

Some children learn to walk and callipers are often used to help. However, many will be in a wheelchair eventually.

Duchenne's Muscular Dystrophy

This is the most common form of childhood dystrophy and affects only boys. The estimated numbers for this type is 1 in 3,500 male births. Most children cope well in the early years of school but by the ages of 8 to 11 the majority will be unable to walk.

If there are associated learning difficulties these are often caused by poor communication and language skills from an early age.

As with other types of dystrophies, there is no cure but the severity of the symptoms has to be assessed for each individual.

Becker Muscular Dystrophy

Again this is a type that affects only males but is milder and progresses far more slowly than Duchenne's MD. This is a fairly rare form and there are often few signs in early childhood other than cramps, being late learning to walk and not being able to run very fast. The symptoms become more evident in the teenage years when a youngster will have difficulty walking fast or climbing stairs.

Again there is no cure at present but with appropriate help those with Becker MD can live to a reasonably old age.

The majority of boys with Becker MD do not have too much trouble in school except that they may not be too successful in PE. A few may have associated learning difficulties but the majority do not.

How can we help?

● Talk to parents – and the child when appropriate
● Do not assume developments will/will not take place but work with the individual
● Think about classroom layout, use of stairs, etc. – access is not just about getting into the building
● Plan AHEAD – the pace of deterioration can vary greatly
● Make full use of help and advice from Physiotherapists and OTs – they can advise on equipment and adaptations
● Ensure a programme of regular exercise – especially swimming
● Use a buddy system
● Foster positive attitudes in others through PSHE
● Make after school clubs accessible to prevent isolation at home
● Make use of computers and when appropriate, computer aids
● Incorporate choice – important for self esteem
● Facilitate staff counselling – remember strong emotions are roused when working with a child with a progressive condition

Muscular Dystrophy Group of Great Britain & Northern Ireland
7-11, Prescott Place, London SW4 6BS
Tel: 020 7720 8055
www.muscular-dystrophy.org

INDIVIDUAL EDUCATION PLAN

Name:	**Start date:**
Year:	**Review date:**
Stage:	**IEP no.:**

Area of concern:		
Strengths:		
Teacher/Support:		

Success Criteria:	**Strategies for use in class:**	**Role of Parent(s)/Carer(s):**

Targets:	**Resources:**	**Agreed by:**
		SENCO:
		Parent(s)/Carer(s):
		Pupil:
		Date:

Glossary

ADD	Attention Deficit Disorder
ADHD	Attention Deficit Hyperactivity Disorder
ASD	Autistic Spectrum Disorder
EBD	Emotional and Behavioural Difficulties/Disorders
EP	Educational Psychologist
EWO	Education Welfare Officer
GLD	Global Learning Difficulties
HI	Hearing Impaired
ICT	Information and Communication Technology
IEP	Individual Education Plan
LSA	Learning Support Assistant
LSS	Learning Support Service
LVA	Low Vision Aids
MLD	Moderate Learning Difficulties
Monocular vision	Sight in one eye only
Myopia	Short-sightedness
Nystagmus	Involuntary movement of the eye
OT	Occupational Therapist
PMLD	Profound and Multiple Learning Difficulties
PRS	Pupil Referral Service
PRU	Pupil Referral Unit
SLT	Speech and Language Therapist
SENCo	Special Educational Needs Co-ordinator
SENSS	Special Educational Needs Support Services
SLD	Severe Learning Difficulties
SLT	Speech and Language Therapist
SpLD	Specific Learning Difficulties (e.g. Dyslexia)
SSA	Special Support Assistant
VI	Visually Impaired

AFASIC

For children and young people with speech and language impairments and their families.
Afasic
2nd Fl.
50-52 Great Sutton St
London EC1V 9HX
Tel: (administration) 020 4909 411
Fax: 020 2512 834
Email: info@afasic.org.uk
The Afasic helpline 0845 355 5577 (local call rate)
http://www.afasic.org.uk/

ACE Centre (Aiding Communication in Education)

The Oxford ACE Centre provides a focus for the use of technology in meeting the needs of young people with physical and communication difficulties.
92 Windmill Road
Headington
Oxford OX3 7DR
Tel: 01865 759 800/810
E-mail: info@ace-centre.org.uk
http://www.ace-centre.org.uk

ADDNET UK

ADDNet is the UK's national website for Attention Deficit (Hyperactivity) Disorder. The purpose of the website is to be a common point of reference for information and intelligent debate on AD/HD in the UK.
ADDNET
Tel: 020 8269 1400
Email: addnet@web-v.co.uk
http://www.btinternet.com/~black.ice/addnet

Advisory Centre for Education (ACE)

An independent national advice centre for parents.
Department A Unit
1C Aberdeen Studios
22 Highbury Grove
London N5 2DQ
http://www.ace-ed.org.uk
Business Line: 020 7354 8318
Freephone: 0808 800 5793
Fax 020 7354 9069
E-mail: ace-ed@easynet.co.uk
http://www.ace-centre.org.uk
Information on exclusions: 0808 8000 327

Alliance for Inclusive Education

The organisation is composed of disabled people, their parents and campaigners. The alliance's aim is to end compulsory segregation in the education system.
ALLFIE Unit 2.
70 South Lambeth
London SW8 1RL
Tel: 020 7735 5277
Fax: 020 7735 3828
http://www.btinternet.com/~allfie/index.html

Asthma and Allergy Information and Research

The objectives of AAIR and those of its parent organisation are to further education and research in asthma and allergic diseases, and it provides support for patients in certain areas.
AAIR
12 Vernon Street
Derby DE1 1FT
Tel: 0116 270 7557 or 0116 270 9338
Email: aair@globalnet.co.uk

http://www.users.globalnet.co.uk/~aair

Autism Independent UK

The Society exists to increase awareness of autism, together with well-established and newly developed approaches in the diagnosis, assessment, education and treatment.
AI UK
199-205 Blandford Avenue
Kettering
Northants NN16 9AT
Tel: 01536 523274
Email: autism@rmplc.co.uk
http://www.autismuk.com

BDA British Dyslexia Institute

The Dyslexia Institute (DI) is an educational charity, founded in 1972, for the assessment and teaching of people with dyslexia and for the training of teachers. For a list of centres around the country please visit:
Email: info@dyslexia-inst.org.uk
http://www.dyslexia-inst.org.uk/contacts.htm

BILD British Institute of Learning Disabilities

BILD provide services that promote good practice in the provision and planning of the health and social care services for people with learning disabilities.
Wolverhampton Road
Kidderminster
Worcestershire DY10 3PP
Tel: 01562 850251
Fax: 01562 851970
E-mail:bild@bild.demon.co.uk

British Epilepsy Association

New Anstey House
Gate Way Drive
Yeadon
Leeds LS19 7XY
Tel: 0113 210 8800
Fax: 0113 391 0300
Tel: 0808 800 5050
Email: helpline@bea.org.uk
http://www.epilepsy.org.uk

British Stammering Association

BSA's mission is to initiate and support research into stammering, to identify and promote effective therapies, offer support to those whose lives are affected by stammering and help teachers to be more responsive to the needs of stammering pupils.
BSA
15 Old Ford Road
London E2 9PJ
Tel: 020 8983 1003 or 020 8983 3591
Email: mail@stammering.org
http://www.stammering.org/homepage.html

CAF Contact a Family

Every day over sixty children in the UK are born or diagnosed with a serious disability and the vast majority of them are cared for at home. Contact a Family (CaF) is the only UK charity providing support and advice to parents whatever the medical condition of their child.
209-211 City Road
London EC1V 1JN
Tel: 020 7608 8720
Fax: 020 7608 8702
E-mail: info@cafamily.org.uk

Centre for Studies on Inclusive Education

CSIE is the Centre for Studies on Inclusive Education. It is a British independent educational charity, a national centre funded mainly by donations. It gives information and advice about inclusive education and related issues.
http://inclusion.uwe.ac.uk/csie/csiehome.htm

The Children's Society

Public Enquiry Point
The Children's Society
Edward Rudolf House
Margery Street
London WC1X 0JL
Tel: 020 7841 4436
Fax: 020 7837 0211
http://www.the-childrens-society.org.uk

Children with Diabetes

The organisation's website aims to develop contact for parents and children who live with diabetes.
http://www.childrenwithdiabetes.co.uk

Conductive Education

Conductive Education is a form of special education and rehabilitation for children and adults with motor disorders.
The National Institute of Conductive Education
Cannon Hill House
Russell Road
Moseley
Birmingham B13 8RD
Tel: 0121 449 1569
Fax: 0121 449 1611
Email: foundation@conductive-education.org.uk
http://www.conductive-education.co.uk

Council for Disabled Children

The Council for Disabled Children promotes collaborative work between different organisations providing services and support for children and young people with disabilities and special educational needs.
http://www.empowernet.org/index.htm

Diabetes UK

The charity works for people with diabetes, funding research, campaigning and helping people live with the condition.
Diabetes UK
Central Office
10 Queen Anne Street
London W1G 9LH
Tel: 020 7323 1531
Email: info@diabetes.org.uk
http://www.diabetes.org.uk/home.htm

Down's Syndrome Association

The Association exists to support parents and carers of people with Down's Syndrome and improve the lives of people with the condition.
The Down's Syndrome Association
155 Mitcham Rd
London SW17 9PG
Tel: 020 8682 4001
Fax: 020 8682 4012
Email: info@downs-syndrome.org.uk
http://www.downsed.org

Dyslexia Institute (DI)

Head Office
133 Gresham Road
Staines
Middlesex TW18 2AJ
Tel: 01784 463 851
Fax: 01784 460 747
Email: http://www.dyslexia-inst.org.uk

Dyspraxia Trust

The Dyspraxia Trust exists to support individuals and families affected by developmental dyspraxia and to increase understanding about it.
The Dyspraxia Foundation
8 West Alley Hitchin
Herts SG5 1EG
Helpline: 01462 454 986
Fax: 01462 455 052
Email: dyspraxiafoundation@hotmail.com
http://www.emmbrook.demon.co.uk/dysprax/homepage.htm

Foundation for People with Learning Disabilities

The Foundation for People with Learning Disabilities works to improve the lives of people with learning disabilities through:
●Funding innovative research and service development projects
●Listening to people with learning disabilities and involving them in its work ●Seeking to influence policy.
The Foundation for People with Learning Disabilities
20/21 Cornwall Terrace
London NW1 4QL
Tel: 020 7535 7400
Email: hmorgan@mhf.org.uk or dthompson@mhf.org.uk

I CAN

I CAN is the national educational charity for children with speech and language difficulties.
I CAN
4 Dyer's Buildings
Holborn
London EC1N 2QP
Tel: 0870 010 4066
Fax: 0870 010 4067
Email: http://www.ican.org.uk/emailus/emailican.html
http://www.ican.org.uk

Independent Panel for Special Education Advice (IPSEA)

IPSEA provides free independent advice; free advice on appealing to the Special Educational Needs Tribunal, including representation when needed and free second professional opinions.
IPSEA
6 Carlow Mews
Woodbridge
Suffolk IP12 1DH
Tel: 0800 018 4016
Advice line: 0800 0184016 or 01394 382814
Tribunal appeals only: 020 8682 0442
General enquiries: 01394 380518
http://www.ipsea.org.uk

MENCAP

Mencap works with people with a learning disability to fight discrimination. It campaigns to ensure that their rights are recognised and that they are respected as individuals.
Mencap
123 Golden Lane
London EC1Y 0RT
Tel: 020 7454 0454
Fax: 020 7696 5540
Email: http://www.mencap.org.uk
http://www.mencap.org.uk

NAGC National Association for Gifted Children

The Association recognises that the needs of gifted children are best met when parents, students, education professionals, schools and colleges are able to share a common forum and gain wider understanding of home/school issues.
National Association for Gifted Children
Elder House
Milton Keynes
Tel: 01908 673677
Fax: 01908 673679
Email: amazingchildren@nagcbritain.org.uk

National Association for Special Educational Needs

The National Association for Special Educational Needs (NASEN) aims to promote the education, training, advancement and development of all those with special educational needs.
NASEN House
4/5 Amber Business Village
Amber Close
Amington
Tamworth B77 4RP
Tel: 01827 311 500
Fax: 01827 313 005
Email: welcome@nasen.org.uk

National Autistic Society

The charity's objective is to provide education, treatment, welfare and care to people with autism and related conditions.
NAS
393 City Road
London EC1V 1NG
Tel: 020 7833 2299 or 020 7833 9666
Email: nas@nas.org.uk

National Children's Bureau

The National Children's Bureau (NCB) is a registered charity which promotes the interests and well-being of all children and young people across every aspect of their lives.
National Children's Bureau
8 Wakley Street
London EC1V 7QE
Tel: 020 7843 6000
Fax: 020 7278 9512
http://www.ncb.org.uk/about.htm

National Deaf Children's Society

The charity is dedicated to supporting all deaf children, young deaf people and their families in overcoming the challenges of childhood deafness.
The National Deaf Children's Society
15 Dufferin Street
London EC1Y 8UR
Switchboard: 020 7490 8656
Fax: 020 7251 5020
Info & Helpline: 020 7250 0123(v/t)
Email: fundraising@ndcs.org.uk
http://www.ndcs.org.uk

National Rathbone Society

Rathbone CI is a national charity and voluntary organisation which believes that progess is possible for all people.
Rathbone CI
4th Floor
Churchgate House
56 Oxford Street
Manchester, M1 6EU
Tel: 0161 236 5358
Fax: 0161 238 6356

OASIS

Office for Advice, Assistance Support and Information on Special needs.
Helpline: 09068 633201
Fax: 01590 622687

Royal National Institute for the Blind RNIB

RNIB's task is to challenge blindness. They challenge the disabling effects of sight loss by providing information and practical services to help people get on with their own lives.
Tel: 0845 766 9999 (UK Helpline callers only)
Tel: 0207 388 1266 (switchboard/overseas callers)
Fax: 0207 388 2034
Email: helpline@rnib.org.uk

Royal National Institute for the Deaf (RNID)

The Royal National Institute for Deaf People (RNID) is the largest charity representing the 8.7 million deaf and hard of hearing people in the UK.
RNID
19-23 Featherstone Street
London EC1Y 8SL
Tel: 0808 808 0123
Fax: 020 7296 8199
Email: informationline@rnid.org.uk
Regional Offices: http://www.rnid.org.uk/html
info_about_rnid_regional_offices.htm

SCOPE

Scope is the national disability organisation whose focus is people with cerebral palsy. Their aim is that disabled people achieve equality: a society in which they are as valued and have the same human and civil rights as everyone else.
Helpline: 0808 800 3333
Email: cphelpline@scope.org.uk
http://www.scope.org.uk

Scottish Dyslexia Association

The SDA provides information and advice to parents, adults, teachers, professional and non-professional people.
SDA
Unit 3
Stirling Business Centre
Wellgreen
Stirling FK8 2DZ
Tel: 01786 446650 or 01786 471235
Email: Dyslexia.scotland@dial.pipex.com
http://www.dyslexia-scotland.org/wee-scot-dyslexia.html

Scottish Society for Autism

The Scottish Society for Autism seeks to ensure the provision of the best education, care, support and opportunities for people of all ages with autism in Scotland.
SSA
Alloa Business Park
Whins Road
Alloa FK10 3SA
Fax: 01259 720051
http://www.autism-in-scotland.org.uk